love and play

By the same author
The Bottom Line Catechism

love and play

BY ANDREW GREELEY

W.H. ALLEN · LONDON
A Howard & Wyndham Company
1984

First published in the USA by The Thomas More Press
First British edition 1984

Copyright © The Thomas More Association 1975

Printed and bound in Great Britain by
Mackays of Chatham Ltd, Kent
for the Publishers, W.H. Allen & Co. Ltd
44 Hill Street, London W1X 8LB

ISBN 0 491 03201 3

"The instinct of fidelity is perhaps the deepest instinct in the great complex we call sex. Where there is real sex there is the underlying passion for fidelity."

D. H. Lawrence

introduction

This volume is an argument for a sustained commitment in the sexual union, or, to use the old phrase, for permanency in marriage. But if I argue for something old, the arguments I use in support of it are, I think, rather new. For I shall contend in this book that playfulness can occur in human relationships, and in particular the sexual relationship, only in an environment created by permanent commitment. Instead of conceding to my adversaries—as most of those who write in the Christian context do—that playfulness and variety are antithetical to the serious business of marriage, I shall argue that authentic playfulness and variety will occur only when there is a strong, sustained commitment between playmates. More than that, I also suggest that given the immense demands placed on the marital relationship today, it will either be playful or it will be considerably less than successful. If sex is not play, it may not be anything at all except occasions for periodic tension release. If marital sex is not playful, then the whole marriage relationship, which is symbolized, reinforced, underwritten and manifested in its sexual dimension, is not viable. An oppressively close relationship such as marital intimacy is either playful or it is intolerable.

The argument is a novel one, I think. It will offend those libertarians who find marital fidelity and permanency a drag. It will also offend that far larger group of human beings who, caught in the grip of the puritan temptation, believe that marriage and sex are far too serious, far too important, and involve far too many responsibilities to allow anything as childish and frivolous as play to enter into the equation. Both groups bear a common assumption: marriage is one thing and play is something else. The one group considers it to be axiomatic that "good" sex (by which they mean "fun" sex) occurs usually only outside marriage. My contention is that they are both wrong. "Good" (fun) sex can only be sustained in a context of a long-term commitment to one's partner, and "good" (moral) sex in marriage can grow only when playfulness characterizes all the dimensions of the intimacy between husband and wife. My argument will not be easily accepted by either side.

There are three basic assumptions that underpin this book. The first is that it is necessary for those Christians who reflect on the meaning of human sexuality to temporarily bracket such questions as pre-, extra-, and comarital sexuality, as well as birth control, divorce, and abortion. These are by no means unimportant issues, but they can only be answered effectively when one has thought through once again what illumination the Christian symbol system can shed on the ambiguity of human sexuality, and what sense of direction it can provide for those who seek to transcend the ambiguities in which they presently find themselves. The resources of theology, philosophy, psychology, and sociology must be brought to bear on the dilemmas of human sexuality so that we can understand better the anguish, the poignance, and the ambiguity of contemporary sexual relationships. We must determine whether any insight, any understanding, can be gained from the Christian symbol system as humankind attempts to cope with these dilemmas.

Secondly, I assume as my principal concern the dilemmas and ambiguities experienced by those who are more or less permanently committed to one another. Despite all the publicity given to alternative sexual forms, most human sex, in fact, still occurs between one man and one woman who have come together in a familial relationship. There is absolutely no reason to think that the situation will change. On grounds of physical and social convenience, if for no other reason, the family is likely to survive. For most people the major problem is not extramarital or premarital or co-marital sex but marital sex. A sexual theory that begins with deviations from the normal (I mean here, "that which is most frequent") will not be applicable to most human beings; and if it is not applicable to most humans, it can hardly be very helpful.

Finally, I assume a very close connection between sexuality and religion. Anthropological and archeological evidence indicate that these two human phenomena are intimately connected. The work of my colleague, William McCready, also suggests that religious world-view and sexual self-definition are acquired in the same process. The challenge of sexuality forces one to fall back on one's basic world-view. One responds to sexual challenge inevitably in terms of one's fundamental interpretive scheme of the cosmos. For even the unreligious, sex is religious—not in the sense perhaps of being "churchy" but surely in the sense of raising questions about the ultimate if not the Ultimate. But if sex and religion are intimately linked, it does not follow that the style with which organized religion has traditionally approached human sexuality is either effective or helpful. All too often religion has been ready to provide answers to sexual problems before the questions were asked. More recently, religion has been providing answers to certain peripheral questions, ignoring more fundamental dilemmas. My assumption is that the role of religion should not be to "answer" sexual questions but to provide illumination and direction to human beings caught in the dilemmas and ambiguities created by their sexual natures. "Man," as Clifford Geertz remarked, "is an animal suspended in the webs of meaning he himself has created." Religion must above all else provide meaning for humankind, and its most important function on the subject of human sexuality is to provide meaning for human sex. Ethical questions, questions about meaning, are surely important, but they are not as important as fundamental meaning, and they cannot be answered until the meaning context has been created. This book is concerned almost solely with the religious meaning of sexuality, not with specific ethical or moral issues. Those I am willing to leave to other writers.

I am therefore not concerned here with the canonical questions of divorce and remarriage for Catholics or the sinfulness of extra or comarital sex. I do not say these are unimportant questions, but they are not the subject of this book. If I argue in favor of sustained sexual commitment, I do so not on canonical or ethical grounds (though I do not reject their importance) but rather on the basis of analysis of the dynamics of sexual playfulness. And if I invoke religion in this book, I do so not to support a canonical or ethical position but because religious symbols will either illumine the dilemmas of sexual playfulness or they will be useless as religious symbols to contemporary humans. Humans will then either find religious symbols that do ratify and reinforce their sexual playfulness or they will stop being playful and settle for lives and sex relationships that are dull and routine.

I intend this book to be a companion volume to my earlier *Sexual Intimacy*. As one who has stumbled more or less by accident into the business of writing about sex, I have been struck by the special demands readers place on an author who discusses sex. Quite simply put, many readers expect you to say everything at once. You may assume nothing, defer nothing to a later chapter, leave out nothing. Many readers begin to argue with you at the first paragraph. I think this is because they feel profoundly threatened by any discussion of sexual intimacy. A book on sex, particularly if it has a religious perspective, is sort of an ink blot into which the reader can project his frustrations, his hatreds, his anger. If one leaves out in any given chapter any reference to children, one is opposed to children. If in another chapter one neglects to mention the frailties and inadequacies of every human relationship, then one is accused of having a "romantic," "idealistic" view of sexuality. It does no good to argue that the matter is treated elsewhere, or that it should be obvious from the context what one's point is. In a book on sex it would seem that nothing is obvious from the context.

When faced with such demands from his readers, the author has two alternatives. He can attempt to say everything at once, qualify every phrase, footnote every sentence, cross reference every paragraph. Or he can assume that what he has to say is intended for reasonably mature adults who are capable of listening to a complex and intricate argument, and who are not waiting to trip him up at the end of every paragraph. In this book I propose to maintain the latter strategy. Sentences must be judged in the context of their paragraphs, paragraphs in the context of the chapter, chapter in the context of the entire book, and this volume in the context of *Sexual Intimacy*. If I am required to repeat everything I said in my first book in order to reassure the reader of my sanity or my orthodoxy or my realism, then I shall be writing that book again. If the reader is trying to pick a fight with me, he will be disappointed to find that I will not fight back. If the reader is willing to listen to me and is curious about the context of my thinking on human sexuality, he might wish to refer to *Sexual Intimacy* either before or after he has read this book.

Thus my argument and my assumptions are laid out clearly at the beginning for all to see. I do not apologize either for the argument or the assumptions. They seem to me to be eminently reasonable.

They are, however, sufficiently different from most Christian writing on sexuality as to be disconcerting to many. Even more disconcerting will be the fact that a committed celibate Catholic priest could presume to write on sexual playfulness. Those who reject ideas and authors on principle because they are disconcerting would be well advised to read no further.

chapter 1

A long time ago, back before the Vatican Council, I was involved in a lengthy discussion with one of the founders of the feminist movement. In 1960 she was surprised to learn that as a Catholic priest I had no problem at all endorsing the goals of feminism (at least in the rhetoric they were stated then). Having seen what the "woman's place is in the home" cultural norms did to well-educated college women in their '30s and '40s, it was difficult for me not to be in favor of the feminist movement even before Pope John endorsed it. The discussion turned somewhat gingerly to the subject of sex. "The trouble with you traditionalists," said my friend, "is that you think sex must be linked with love. I quite agree with the impressive

Christian vision of marriage, but I don't think that sex needs to be limited to marriage. Modern men and women have discovered that sex can be play, and it does not necessarily have to involve love. You can enjoy sex with strangers, casual acquaintances, the person down the street without there being any psychological intimacy involved."

My friend was deeply committed to her own marriage, and while she and her husband would not define themselves exactly as Christians, she was still willing to admit that the Christian ideal of marriage and the Christian concept of the relationship between sex and love were compelling. If sex were linked with love, then, she conceded, the result was almost inevitably something that looked like marriage. But sex didn't have to be linked with love; it could also be play, and play was casual, spontaneous, freewheeling, open-ended.

I responded with what was the more or less approved "Cana line" of the day: human sexuality was a serious business; sustained personal relationships required depth, maturity, commitment; shallow, superficial sexual encounters were unrewarding and frustrating. Marriage was a serious attempt to build a common life together, of which sexuality would be a part, an important part, but not the only part. Frivolous and casual relationships might have a short-run psychological payoff, but in the long term they would be harmful and counterproductive. My friend neither agreed nor disagreed; she simply continued to insist that sex need not involve love, and that the discovery (or rediscovery) of the playful elements of sex had changed the entire picture of contemporary human sexuality.

A lot has happened since 1960. Hedonism, which existed in those days as the sophisticated version of such sexologists as the Ellises (Havelock and Albert) and in the adolescent variety of the then emerging "*Playboy* Philosophy," has become a popular and widely heralded sexual theory. Wife-swapping, group marriages, alternative marriages, open marriages, "comarital" sex are all hailed as part of the sexual revolution and propagated by some with the dedicated missionary fervor of those who believe they are the wave of the future. We may not remember that hedonism is a very old theory. We ignore the bizarre argument of some of the neohedonists that spouse-swapping or group sex reinforces the bonds of middle-class marriage. We rarely observe that many of the advocates of hedonism are dreadfully serious, unattractive people. We never mind that much of the new hedonism is an exercise in chauvinism, with males striving to act out their adolescent fantasies by pressuring their wives into experiments (See Gilbert Bartel, *Group Sex*; New York: New American Library, 1971). And we never notice that the neohedonists represent what is certainly a very small segment of the population. The critical point is that they have taken the initiative in proclaiming the importance of variety and play in sexual relationships. However, we concede too much when we allow them to propound that variety and play in sexual relationships should be sought with a number of different people.

My response to my feminist friend in 1960 was an example of that excessive concession. At no point in the discussion did I deny that casual, transient, "spontaneous" relationships could provide playfulness and variety. I accepted as a given the dichotomy between the serious business of marriage and sexual playfulness. I assumed that playfulness was shallow and superficial. In the face of such argumentation the hedonists will surely sweep the field of battle because it has already been yielded to them.

A couple of months ago I encountered a "with it" marriage counselor (of vague Catholic antecedents) who repeated the argument I heard from the protofeminist back in 1960. This time I was ready.

"Do your children [both of them under ten] like to play?" I asked.

"Well of course they do."

"And do they play with strangers, casual acquaintances, people they don't care about?"

"That's different," she said, somewhat lamely.

The trouble with "sex as play" philosophy, as articulated in its adolescent statement in *Playboy* and now *Playgirl* or in its much more sophisticated version of so-called "scientific" experts, is not that it misunderstands sex. The trouble is that it misunderstands play. Sex is a game, all right, and an uproariously funny one at that; but the "play" crowd has long since forgotten what a game is.

Sex is either playful or it becomes a difficult burden, an obligation, a tension release that produces only minimal satisfaction. A marriage is either a playful relationship, a relationship between playmates (understood here as "mates who play"), or it is an intolerable version. The tango in "Last Tango in Paris" was a dance of death. It was a caricature of the playmate relationship of the *Playboy* Philosophy. It represented, sometimes crudely and tastelessly, the loneliness and despair that lie just beneath the surface of shallow, selfish hedonism. The merit of the picture—and it was not, in my judgment, much of an artistic success— was that it portrayed the loneliness and despair of a sexual relationship without depth, without commitment. The tango was anything but playful.

But neither are many marriages. Depth they may have—particularly when there are children involved—and passion they may generate, but lightness, merriment, playfulness are too often absent. Watch closely, for example, the electricity between the husband and wife when they move from one modality to another. They enter a cocktail or dinner party. There had been a frantic rush at the end of the day to take care of the children, dress for the party, get into the car to arrive no more than a half hour late. Tensions, conflicts, desires, passions, frustrations build up in the frantic rush to get out of the house and to the party. When they enter the room it is almost as though they have interrupted a conversation and must now put on hastily a new set of masks. There may have been no argument, no overt conflict, no serious discussion even during the preparations and trip to the party. Still there was a powerful electricity between them as they came through the door, and on that electrical current there were many messages: love, affection, frustration, anger, hatred, desire, resentment, conflict, weariness, hope. The current is powerful and cannot be disconnected. They cannot live with each other in an easy, casual fashion, yet they surely cannot live without each other either. (Although as the children grow up, the marriage will likely go through a severe crisis and may even end.)

Or imagine the husband and wife stepping into a hotel elevator in the morning. In the tense silence between them, the electrical current alternates back and forth with great intensity. When they are home there is rarely time for interaction in the morning; they must get the kids and themselves off to their respective tasks. But in the unfamiliar, cramped quarters of the hotel room and with the prospect of breakfast, indeed a whole day together, the ordinary context of their relationship is temporarily shattered. Desire may be heightened but also frustration, resentment, and discontent. It is as though the lines were overloaded; there is so much being exchanged silently between the two of them. Now in the presence of the embarrassed third party there is silence, tension, and resentment charging the air.

Intimacy in marriage can be oppressively close. It can take on the inevitability of a soggy, humid summer day or a bitter winter's snowstorm. One is simply caught up in it; you cannot enjoy it, you cannot escape from it. The relationship is intricate, complex, subtle, powerful, demanding, and occasionally rewarding, of course. What is missing is a characteristic that might not eliminate any of the messages passing from one to the other but might well transform the significance of those messages. That element is play. One encounters marital playfulness occasionally, and the difference between married playmates and other couples is so striking that one apprehends it immediately. When a husband and wife come into the cocktail party they seem to be laughing with and at each other. Their jests, some of them secret and almost embarrassingly private, bounce back and forth throughout the evening. They enjoy being at the party together, and whatever other messages are on the electrical charges, the message of mutual enjoyment is paramount. They may fight like cats and dogs, but they seem to enjoy that too.

When you intrude into their privacy by being on the elevator with them in the morning, you cannot miss the fact that behind their silence is a teasing, laughing amusement. The strange, unfamiliar confines of the hotel room for such a couple are not an oppression but an opportunity; and the electricity leaping back and forth between them suggests that they are not merely husband and wife, they are playmates.

But what is play and how do we become playful? That we have to ask this question is evidence that we have forgotten what it was like. The child does not need a definition of play, and no one has to teach him how to be playful. Play is a world unto itself, a game with its own rules, its own parameters, its own constraints. It is real, indeed, terribly real; but it is quite distinct from the mundane world of everyday events. The child does not confuse his game with the rest of life. The boundary lines are firm, but within those boundaries the rules of the game replace the rules of the real world. His game is competitive, imaginative, festive, fantastic; it is intricate, subtle, involved. It is played only with friends, with those you trust, with those you care about. Strangers are not welcomed into the game—not until they stop being strangers. The game is spontaneous, but it is also disciplined. Any spontaneity that breaks the rules of the game will destroy it. The game is fun, but it is also serious; it is competitive, but the rules must be strictly observed.

Children can play because they have the fundamental capacity to create worlds of fantasy and festivity that are "real" but distinct from the other real world. From the perspective of the world whose reality is mundane, the world of play is imaginative and perhaps even "unreal." But from the perspective of someone playing the game, the imaginative world is not unreal at all; it just has a different kind of reality.

The tragedy of growing up, for most of us at any rate, is that we lose this imaginative capacity to create a world of play. Even our games are not festive and fantastic but are invaded by the dreadful mundaneness of the ordinary world. Compare nine-year-olds playing baseball (at least the game removed from that awful creation of the adult world, Little League) with their fathers' golf game. Both age groups play to win, but there is a lightness and a frolic in the game of the nine-year-olds that their fathers rarely match. Winning is important in the game, but when it is over it is no longer important. For his father, on the other hand, competitiveness frequently becomes a way of "proving" his masculinity; winning is a deadly serious business. Unlike the child the adult is incapable of excluding the mundane from the playful.

In the ideal maturation process exactly the opposite should occur. Adults ought to permit the festivity and fantasy of play to carry over and transform their mundane lives. In other words, maturity means becoming more than children rather than less. The playful adult is the person who has kept alive his childhood capacity for dreams and celebration, and has developed the skills required to permit those dreams and celebrations to give shape and color and tone to the totality of his life. For such an adult sex is one of the greatest of games, and the festivity and fantasy, the imagination and resourcefulness which mark the game played in the bedroom with one's spouse simply cannot be contained there. It should permeate the rest of the relationship and the rest of life. Imaginative, challenging, vigorous foreplay precedes sex; but sex in itself becomes foreplay for the rest of life.

Play, of course, is relational. Children may occasionally play by themselves, and they certainly spin elaborate game fantasies without the help of other children. But these fantasies usually involve other people even if they are only make-believe. The child playing by himself rapidly tires of the game, and seeks out a friend to invite into his dream world. For a child, playful relationships are relatively easy to create, because neither he nor his friend requires much depth to be able to sustain a game. But adult playful relationships are devilishly difficult to create and sustain. A child need not risk much of himself by inviting another child into his fantasies, his dreams, his celebrations, his festivities. But an adult, presumably admitted to the rigorous demands of the mundane world, exposes himself quite completely when he invites another to share fantasy and celebration with him. "Serious," businesslike, responsible relationships come relatively easily; playful ones are difficult if not impossible for most adults. Sex, then, must necessarily be serious, businesslike, responsible. It cannot really be a game, and even casual, transient sex quickly becomes serious despite its superficiality—indeed, probably because of it. One must absolutely and imperatively enjoy casual sex, for if it isn't fun it isn't anything, and the whole thing will be totally devoid of meaning.

It is precisely on the subject of meaning that religion inevitably intervenes in the search for sexual playfulness. The child does not doubt that playfulness is possible. Nor does he doubt that it has a point; he does not need religious symbols to give him the courage to break out of the mundane world into the world of fantasy. While he draws a sharp line between the mundane and the fantastic, it is not one that gives superiority to one world or the other. But the adult, caught up as he is in the cares, the responsibilities, the weariness, the routine of daily life, is not at all sure that it is safe to "pretend," or to admit that that "let's pretend" world might also be real. The child goes off to the land of Oz with almost reckless ease even though it doesn't really exist. And when he finally succumbs to disbelief in that magical land, the possibility of play is gone from his life. It is, as we shall see in this book, not easy to develop a sustained playful relationship with one's sexual partner. One can go through the mechanics of foreplay, lasting somewhere between fifteen minutes and one half hour for the typical American couple (according to a study limited, alas, to young college graduates), without the interlude's being anything more than a perfunctory physiological routine. There are obviously some organs of the opposite sex that almost demand that we play with them, and once we do play with them, delightful reactions occur both in our partner and in ourselves. To engage in such activity with a modicum of efficiency is not all that difficult, though a surprisingly large number of married couples are not even capable of advancing that far. To turn the foreplay interlude—that most critical of transitions between ordinary life and orgasm—into an exercise of relaxed, confident, creative, spontaneous mutual fantasy and celebration requires all kinds of skills and sensitivities that seem to be in short supply in the population. And to create a context for sexual relationship for which the foreplay transition is both a symbol and a continuation and a reinforcement takes practice, discipline, patience, perseverance. Many would prefer not to commit themselves.

In other words, foreplay becomes play—as a child understands the word—only in the context of a relationship that is already characterized by qualities of adult playfulness that are hard to acquire, and which many people feel are foolish and unnecessary.

Sex cannot be playful if one does not believe in the possibility of play in one's life, and many of us do not believe in that possibility. In response to my previous book, *Sexual Intimacy*, I received many angry letters from people (mostly women) whose lives were blighted by suffering and sorrow, some of it clearly of their own making. In a grim world of sickness, noisy children, miscarriages, drunken husbands, employment worries, frustrations, disillusionments, and disappointments can one seriously believe that play is possible, desirable, or necessary? Sex is an obligation, a routine, an interlude. To demand of people who have suffered through and from sex that it be a game is irrational and unjust. One cannot demand anything of anyone in these matters, but if the question is whether play is possible and whether sex can be playful there is, I think, a very clear answer in the Christian symbol system: play is indeed possible and is in fact the only adequate response to the Christian message of joy preached in the Gospel.

If play is possible for adults and if enjoyment of fun and games is an appropriate response to the Good News we have heard, then sex should become fun and games. Our relationship with our sexual partner ought not to be one of tolerance or obligation or long-suffering acceptance but rather one of sport, delight, and playfulness. To those who say it is no longer possible for them, one must express sympathy—and perhaps a bit of skepticism. Of course they are best able to judge their own cases, but still it must be said that playful sex is not only a legitimate ideal for Christians, it is also an especially appropriate response to the illumination radiated by the Christian symbol system.

In a somber, dull, stodgy, humorless world it might be wrong for sex to be playful, but in a world of joy, confidence, and eager expectation there is no reason for sex not to be playful, and many reasons for it to become an exercise in joy, festivity, celebration, and fantasy. To put the matter somewhat differently, when two sexual partners are firmly committed to each other and seek to become playmates, their efforts are ratified and reenforced by the Christian symbol system, which tells them that such playful joy is an appropriate response to the wheeling, dealing, playful Holy Spirit. When a couple decides—and it is usually an implicit decision—that their sexual relationship should be restrained, constrained, routine, and carefully controlled, they cannot justify it in terms of a religious symbol system. Christian lovers dance and play together because they believe that life, for all its tragedy, is still ultimately a comedy, indeed, a comic, playful dance with a passionately loving God.

It all depends on what meaning we wish to impart to a phenomenon. Clifford Geertz, in one brilliant essay, poses the question of what the wink of an eye means. It is, after all, only a physiological reflex—a nervous quirk, a response to a bright light—but it also might be a laugh, a suggestion, a subtle message. But what is the message? Does it mean "Don't believe me," or "Laugh with me," or

"I would like to sleep with you," or "That person is crazy, isn't he?" The physiological movement of nerves and muscles is the same, but what that reaction means to the one who emits it and the one who perceives it depends entirely on their shared interpretation of an eyelid twitch. One can, as Geertz points out, put almost any meaning into it from the most shallow to the most profound.

If such be the case with a blink of an eye, how much more is it true of sexual intercourse! Two people come together in a context in which they have temporarily shut themselves off from the rest of the world. They remove their clothes, they enjoy looking at each other's body, they caress and manipulate one another, becoming increasingly more vigorous and direct in their mutual stimulation. The bodies join, they twist and turn, there are spasms, convulsions, and then relaxation—five minutes, fifteen minutes, forty-five minutes and it is over. But what does the event mean? Is it an obligation? An economic exchange (either in a house of prostitution or in a suburban home)? Is it an interlude that one or both partners experience with loathing and disgust? Is it a routine and absent-minded episode? Is it a burst of spontaneous passion? Is it a brief encounter between two people who will never see each other again? Is it part of a great game between two people who have become specialists in playing with one another? Is it a celebration of a relationship which, for all its difficulties and problems, is basically characterized by joyous love? Is it a response not only to the attractiveness of the other's body and person but also to a basically benign and attractive cosmos? Is it an act of play celebrated in the midst of a universe that both lovers believe to be benign and gracious or in an oppressive and absurd universe which can punish and destroy? Have these two lovers created for themselves a world of mutual fantasy and festivity, a world in which they are able to be always a surprise and delight to one another? Or are they grim, determined, serious people desperately seeking that kind of orgasm which they have read in the sex manuals is a proof of their success in lovemaking as a man and a woman? Or are they two angry, hateful, punitive people, who are taking out their vindictiveness towards the cosmos and the rest of the human race by tormenting one another?

The list of questions could be endless. Whether the encounter of man and woman is a playful response to a playful universe or not depends ultimately on whether they believe in the possibility of play, hope, and joy. They can interpret their sexual encounters in almost any way they want; how they interpret them will have a profound influence on both the quality of each encounter and their entire relationship with each other.

There are two reasons why sexual play cannot be something casual and "spontaneous." First, as even fifteen minutes of observation of children at play would indicate, play by its very nature is not casual. It may not be serious the way it is in the mundane world, but within its own context the game has norms of seriousness which are indispensable. Doing whatever one wants, or doing what comes naturally, or "letting it all hang out" destroys the game.

Secondly, whether sex is playful or not depends ultimately on what meaning we give to our sexual encounter. Questions of meaning in human life are never easy, simple, casual ones. We can interpret our sex as playful, and within the context of that interpretation we can expend the energies required to see that it becomes and remains playful. But before we can make this interpretation we have to resolve questions about ourselves, about the other, about the human race, and about the cosmos. These issues are anything but casual or trivial.

Paradoxically, play must be very serious, but it will be destroyed by seriousness. As G. K. Chesterton put it, "The more serious the situation, the more playful the Christian must be." One watches an accomplished entertainer like Ann-Margaret (and one can like her or not—I confess to finding her resistible) and has to admit that here is an extraordinarily vivid, dynamic, and spectacular entertainer. She gyrates, cavorts, and bellows around the stage and through the audience with an ease, a confidence, and apparent spontaneity that is characteristic of the true professional. Ann-Margaret is an absolute expert at playing with an audience. Yet one can tell without even reading her publicity that an immense amount of serious preparation, practice and discipline went into her act, and that she must be deadly serious about her profession. Each TV special can make or break the career of any performer, particularly that of any whose act depends on torch-singing and grinding dance. It is precisely because the special is so serious and she is so serious about her career that her performance must give the appearance of being relaxed, casual, spontaneous. Only discipline, practice, and self-control can enable one to be playful in deadly serious situations. The amateur falls apart and becomes serious in serious moments; the professional becomes brilliantly relaxed, self-possessed, creative. If our sex is to be playful we must become professional.

Most marriages are both too serious to be playful and not serious enough. They are too serious because the burdens, the responsibilities, the discouragements, the frustrations of life make the relationship so heavy, so oppressive that there is no room for fantasy and celebration. And they are not serious enough, because neither partner has expended the effort, the energy, and the discipline or the perseverence, the patience, to become professional in the skills that this particular relationship requires. Hedonism quite properly indicts the oppressive seriousness, but it does not even begin to understand the reasons why a serious commitment to growth of a relationship is indispensable for the play that hedonism superficially exults.

The blink of the eye is subject to an infinite variety of interpretations, but more complex human activities are less malleable. There are a wide variety of possible interpretations for sexual encounter, but most of them are either gracious or malign. The overwhelming pleasure of orgasm and the fierce physical self-revelation involved are either the hint of something much better or the ultimate absurdity of a punitive universe. If the former is the case, then play is possible. It is the rare husband and wife who do not experience at least the intuition that much more is possible in lovemaking and in the totality of life together and, indeed, in the totality of life itself. When two bodies are pressed together, the flesh soft and smooth, the organs firm and demanding, the passion wild to the point of fury, the rhythms of union building to a crescendo, they are, however temporarily, translated out of the mundane world into one where playfulness seems not only possible but imperative. As they hold each other tight and close, they experience—however fleetingly and however rarely—the hint of an explanation, an explanation of themselves, their sexuality, their love, their life, and of the universe.

The critical question is whether that hint ought to be taken seriously or brushed aside when they return, all too quickly, to the ordinary, mundane world. On some occasions when they are making love to one another they find themselves carried away into a celebration. Ought one to take seriously the possibility that there is a great deal to celebrate?

chapter 2

There are a number of painful dilemmas built into the structure of contemporary marital sexuality. On the one hand there is a tremendous biological urge for sexual union reinforced by the psychological theory that says such union is good and healthy. On the other hand there is the friction, conflict, tension, and strain that necessarily builds up between two human beings who are forced to live together in close and intimate personal relations. Sexual yearnings draw a man and woman together; interpersonal strains force them apart.

At a deeper level there is the conviction that interpersonal relationships, in particular, marriage, are the major source of life satisfaction available to human beings in the contemporary world. A tremendous amount of emotional resources are necessarily involved in seeking marital satisfaction, but so much time and effort must be expended on the difficulties of building a life together that there seems little left over for enjoying the results of a common life. Self-fulfillment is the goal of marriage, but the work necessary to hold the marriage together seems to preclude the possibility of much fulfillment.

There is, then, the serious business of marriage, that of building a life together; and then there is the excitement, the adventure of sexual exploration and play. The two do not seem to fit together very well. Indeed it almost seems as though one must choose, and eventually, for most people, the choice is the common life rather than playfulness. Sexual adventure outside the common life is a solution for very few; it is time-consuming and inconvenient and quickly becomes psychologically painful.

The choices seem clear enough. One either builds a common life without romance or pursues romance without the common life. For the young, the latter alternative seems more attractive; for the older—particularly after the trauma of a divorce—the former seems to be less painful, less traumatic. The risky compromise in between, in which common life characterizes one relationship and playfulness another, is so frustrating in the long run when one relationship or the other either goes sour or they impinge on one another to such a degree that both relationships become intolerable. One cannot have playful adventurous, exciting, festive, fantastic sex with one person and at the same time build strong, stable, supportive family life with another.

But how can the conflicts, the tensions, the responsibilities, the burdens, the financial and administrative difficulties, constant problems with the children—all those things that constitute the warp and woof of family living—coexist with playfulness? At the end of a human life, or on anniversary days, one looks back on the struggles and strains, the successes and failures, the defeats and the accomplishments of a common life and realizes that these are what human existence is all about. One may have had to give up some of one's dreams and ideals, but the sacrifice seems worth the effort. Life is a serious business, after all. One may have youthful adventures and perhaps one or two more in mature adulthood, but these are of a different and substantially lesser order of being than is the common life one has built with one's spouse and children.

Or at least so it seems.

The hedonists argue that such a life of bourgeois respectability is dull, weary, and dead. Human beings, they insist, are playful creatures by nature, and they repress the festive, the fantastic, the creative genius, the imaginative, fun-loving, pleasure-seeking elements of their lives at the risk of becoming substantially less than human. The drab,

unexciting, unmysterious, unadventurous suburban middle-class marriage may be an efficient
economic and social unit, the hedonists tell us; it
may be well suited for the production and con-
sumption of wealth and the education of children,
but it necessarily represses much of the human
personality and stagnates human development and
growth. Culture, art, religion, poetry, mysticism,
we are informed, all require that humans be able
to break away, at least intermittently, from the
mundane, the routine, the ordinary, and the commonplace. The stodgy, mediocre American family
life, they insist, is a caricature of human sexuality.
The furtive, episodic, and unfulfilling release of
sexual tension characteristic of such marriages is
in its own way even more obscene than sexual
promiscuity. Sex without play, without delight,
without festivity is, they say, the ultimate in sexual immorality.

The hedonists have a point, though, like all her-
etics, they confuse part of the truth with the whole
of it. Forced to choose between playfulness and
somberness, authentic Christianity must choose
the former, for a Christian believes (along with
Plato) that man is a plaything of God; creation was
an act of sport, of playfulness, of creative fantasy
and imagination. The Book of Wisdom presents
the divine Logos playfully cooperating in God's
frolicsome creation of the world. Or, as one of the
old Latin versions translates the Greek, *"Jucunda-*

bar ante faciem aeius in omni tempore, cum lae-
taretur orbe perfecto." ("I was playful before his
face all the time when he was rejoicing over the
completing of the earth.")

St. Gregory of Nazianzen put the same thought
into one of his poems:

> For the Logos on high plays
> Stirring the whole cosmos back and forth as
> he wills into being shapes of every kind.

A contemporary scripture scholar, Cornelius a
Lapide notes of the Logos that, "In the dewy fresh-
ness and the springtime beauty of his eternal
youth, he eternally enacts a game before his
Father."

Hugo Rahner, in his book, *Man at Play* (Herder
and Herder, 1967, from which I have lifted the
previous quotations), argues that only when we
understand the notion of a *Deus ludens* (a playing
God) can we understand the notion of *Homo ludens*. Life is joy and sorrow, comedy and tragedy,
defeat and victory. Existence is joyful because it
is secure in God; it is tragic because it is free, and
from freedom comes risk and peril. Man, says
Father Rahner, "is really always two men in one.
He is a man with an easy gaiety of spirit, one might
almost say a man of spiritual elegance, a man who
feels himself to be living in invincible security;
but he is also a man of tragedy, a man of laughter

and tears, a man indeed of gentle irony, for he sees through the tragically ridiculous mask of the game of life and has taken the measure of the cramping boundaries of our earthly existence."

Our play, then, is both a celebration of our confidence and an ironic recognition of the fragility of our existence. Rahner quotes with approval the eloquent words of Plotinus: "After all, things at play, play only because of their urge to attain to the vision of God, whether they are the seriousness of the grown man or the play of a child."

Rahner also sees anticipation of the Christian vision of *Deus ludens* and *Homo ludens* in the choral ode in *The Frogs:*

> Let me never cease throughout the day
>   to play, to dance, to sing.
> Let me utter many a quip
> Let me also say much meant in earnest
> And if my playing and mockery be worthy
>   of thy feast
> Let me be crowned with the garland of
>   victory.

The Christian cannot help but agree with the hedonist critique of a life that is mundane and dull. When humans become so rooted in the problems, the cares, the responsibilities of daily life that they cannot break away for festivity and fantasy, they have cut themselves off from both the tragic and comic dimensions of human existence. As Robert

Neale says in his book, *In Praise of Play,* "He who cannot play, cannot pray. He who cannot escape from the responsibilities of work simply will not have time to lift up his head and confront the cosmos and its creator" (Harper & Row, 1969).

This volume is not intended to be a defense of the theology of play. Nor is it an argument justifying the playful dimensions of the human personality and the playful aspects of human existence. I intend to assume that play is justified and indeed indispensable for humankind. I intend to assume that the hedonistic critique of unplayful sex is valid. I take it as axiomatic that a sexual relationship from which all imagination and celebration has been removed is not a Christian relationship. It may very well be an admirable, praiseworthy, responsible, sensible way to live; the religion that underpins it—stoicism—has always been impressive, but it is not Christianity. Stoic sexuality—puritanism—is not Christian sexuality no matter how much it may claim to be.

But if Christianity agrees with hedonism and its criticism of the unplayful life, it must side with the Stoics in their criticism of the shallow, superficial, rootless life of the hedonist. When the Stoic says romance is not possible if a common life is to be built, the Christian enthusiastically endorses the hedonist's position that life without romance is hardly life at all. But when the hedonist then contends that romance is to be sought outside the common life, the Christian must also dissent. As I argue in this book, romance apart from the common life cannot survive for very long.

The common life is an absolutely indispensable context for playfulness. Playfulness in its turn is absolutely indispensable to keep the common life from becoming intolerably oppressive. There is surely strain between playfulness and the common life; strain is part of the human condition, that admixture of comedy and tragedy, joy and sorrow, life and death. But one does not solve the problem of strain between two polarities by repressing one or the other part. One can balance a common life and playfulness only when one has powerful convictions that such a balance is possible. And the Christian, being possessed of religious symbols that generate such convictions, ought to be equipped for the struggle to balance the mundane, the ordinary and the fantastic, the commonplace and the playful, the routine and the imaginative. Most of those who profess to be Christian may be unaware of the fact, but it is in that balancing act that one finds the essence of Christian life and, necessarily, the essence of Christian sexuality. Christians are not, of course, the only ones who have grasped this insight. Father Rahner's quotations of some of the Greeks make it clear that others have seen it too. All that can be said is that the Christian vision of a *Deus ludens*, a playful God, gives them an extremely powerful religious symbol to reinforce their search for a mixture of responsibility and playfulness, seriousness and frolic. We may continue to be dull, but to the extent that we are dull we are false to the belief we profess.

Two convictions are necessary: (1) Sex has a built-in strain toward playfulness, which can be resisted only at the price of reducing the payoffs and the binding power of sexual intimacy; (2) Playfulness cannot survive unless it is rooted in the context of a long-term, sustained, total human relationship, one underpinned by the fundamental conviction of the possibility of hope and of love.

The strain toward playfulness in sexuality ought to be self-evident. Indeed most of those who contend that there is little room in life for sexual playfulness do so not on the grounds that sex is inherently unplayful but rather that the other obligations and responsibilities of life make it necessary to limit and restrain sex's playful propensities. If a man and woman would spend as much time playing with one another as their sexual instincts impel them, nothing else would be done.

Most sexual partners are well aware that they impose severe restraints on their sexual exchanges. Remote preparation, foreplay, lovemaking itself are all restrained compared to what they might be. Such restraints are explained on the grounds of no time or energy, other commitments, or even concern for the sensitivities of the other partner. Honesty might lead them to add that fear, uncertainty, shame, and punitiveness are additional motivations for the limitations of their sexual playfulness.

All human events are necessarily limited and constrained. I am not arguing here for the abandonment of restraints. I merely point out that sexual partners know that they could easily be far more playful in their interchanges than they are in fact. At the end of an episode that has been at best undistinguished both the man and woman know that if they had been a little more sensitive, a little more patient, a little more considerate, a little more demanding, a little more challenging, a little more imaginative, the payoff would have been much greater. The man may well think to himself, in effect, "If I had been more affectionate when I came home, more tender through the supper hour, more cheerful during the evening, more fervent, less restrained and inhibited during the intercourse itself, the results would have been more satisfying for the two of us." If she had been more seductive, warmer, more enticing, more insistent on her own pleasure, more aggressive, more unrestrained in her reactions, both of them would have less guilt about the relative failure of the sexual interlude. It would have been relatively easy to make much more of the episode, but they were both distracted, preoccupied, perhaps resentful and frustrated. What might have been a great event was only a mediocre one.

Even on those occasions when the sexual encounter is uninhibited, unrestrained and genuinely
ecstatic, the man and woman are still aware—and
perhaps more poignantly so—not merely that they
could much more frequently experience such
mutual pleasure but also that it is relatively easy
to go beyond where they were even when the
satisfaction was great indeed. There are so many
things one can do psychologically and physically;
there are so many ways that sex can be enjoyed;
there are so many ways one can turn on one's
partner and be turned on by that partner. The
point is that not all sex must be perfect; despite
the left-wing Puritans, in our limited and imperfect human condition that will never be the case.
But most men and women know that they are
capable of much more in their sexual lives than
they permit themselves to experience and that
there is immense room for growth and development in sexual pleasure and playfulness if they
can find the time, the energy, and the courage and
honesty to seek such development.

There are, of course, some people for whom
this awareness of the possibility of development
does not seem to exist. Their sexual lives have
become so narrow, so cramped, so furtive, so inhibited, so anxious that they take their pleasure
with haste, embarrassment, guilt, quickly walling
off the experience from the rest of their lives. The
feel of finger on flesh for them does not indicate
new possibilities for their development but new

and unacceptable feelings to be quickly denied.

Sex, then, can be playful; indeed for most people it can be more playful than it is. That part of the argument is not difficult to make. But the other aspect of sex, the one that concerns us throughout most of this book, is that playfulness requires permanence, or at least a sustained commitment.

The decisive issue in arguing with the hedonists is whether playfulness is something natural, spontaneous, casual; or, put differently, whether playfulness in its apparent spontaneity is something that comes easily and effortlessly or whether it is rather a skill acquired only by patience, practice, and commitment. The professional "player," the basketball star, figure skater, the chess champion, TV comedian, Las Vegas nightclub singer and dancer all give the impression of ease and spontaneity; but we know that they are able to appear relaxed, casual, and spontaneous about what they do because they have sharpened their skills and disciplined their responses through long, rigorous, patient practice. The professional basketball guard spots an opening and dribbles through it to the basket with no conscious reflection not because such behavior is "natural" but because long years of effort and practice have so disciplined him that he is able to spot such situations and respond to them with a quickness that is so unreflective that it seems natural, spontaneous, and instinctive. Similarly a professional quarterback comes to the line of scrimmage, glances over the opposition's defense, and changes his play, calling an audible signal to take advantage of a weakness he sees in a defensive alignment. Afterwards he would be hard put to say exactly what his line of reasoning was. That he can size up and react to such a situation is not a sign that he is doing something natural or instinctive or spontaneous but that he is a disciplined, practiced professional.

Skill at any kind of game, then, requires patience, practice, perseverance, commitment. Such characteristics are especially needed when the game requires a partner. The pro quarterback and a wide receiver must play together for a couple of years before they are so sensitive to one another's moves, skills, attitudes, instincts that they fit together like a perfectly balanced, delicate mechanism. A good wide receiver, dashing down the field and noting the sudden switch in the defensive situation, *knows* what his quarterback is likely to do in reaction. Without pausing a moment to reflect or changing the speed of his run he adjusts to what he expects his passer to do. Similarly the quarterback can feel and sense how the receiver will react to the situation. It may be a broken play, but still the ball will be right there on target just as the receiver arrives in place to catch it.

A doubles tennis team, a figure skating duo, accomplished bridge partners, astronauts on a mission, a jazz combo, a symphony conductor and a soloist (for Chicago it is George Solti and Vladimir Ashkenazy)—all these teams are held together by subtle, complex, sophisticated relationships in which cues and signals are given and exchanged so quickly, so adroitly, so unselfconsciously that even those who are communicating with each other would be hard put to say how the communication took place. But they have acquired their skills of exchange, cooperation, mutual sensitivity, adjusting one response to another only through a long period of hard, patient, persistent practice.

Just imagine two figure skaters trying to leap about on the ice without ever having practiced together. The audience would surely see at least one serious accident before the night is over.

It is also necessary that there be at least some kind of interpersonal trust and affection between the members of such teams. They don't have to be the closest of friends off the playing field (though in the case of Butch Cassidy and the Sundance Kid of the Miami Dolphins or Gale Sayers and Brian Piccolo of the Chicago Bears we can see that such friendships do develop). What is necessary is that they like each other and respect each other enough so that the success of their joint venture becomes more important than discharging individual resentments. If a quarterback is angry at a wide receiver who is getting more publicity than he is, the passes are likely to be ever so slightly overthrown —without even the quarterback's intending it. It would be very risky indeed to be a member of an aerial acrobatic team towards whom other members had deep and abiding resentments. Playing together, in other words, requires practice, cooperation, respect, and some modicum of trust and friendship. One must fit one's patterns to the other's, while the other is at the same time adjusting his. This is a complicated, intricate, subtle, challenging, and ultimately rewarding process; and this is what play is all about.

Even play among children requires that the fellow players make adjustments to the rhythms of each other's play—one that most children make easily and effortlessly. The child who refuses to make the adjustments will either pick up his marbles and leave the playground or find himself quietly but firmly excluded from future games. A "spoilsport" is precisely one who is not willing to merge his own abrasive individuality into the team effort.

But note well that individuality is not lost but enhanced through cooperative effort. A good quarterback looks better when he has a good receiver; a good bridge player operates more effectively with a skillful partner; a good tennis player's talent is enhanced by a skillful partner; a good comedian can be made even funnier by an adroit straightman. One may lose some of oneself by commitment to the joint cooperative effort of the Game, but one also gains something new. "He who loses his life shall find it."

Good play is both elegant and fun, but the elegance comes from skill and self-discipline (as in a complex water ballet) and not from spontaneous exhibitionism. Fun comes not from doing whatever you want to do but from meshing one's talents and skills in intricate nuance with those of others. When Bobby Orr drives the puck by a goalie he has a good deal more fun than when he fails to score, but his ability to succeed so often comes from both his individually honed skills and the practiced discipline of team play.

Play, then, results from practiced ease. Lots of young men grow up with good arms and good eyes and good coordination, but the great quarterbacks are those who can begin with such raw talent and can discipline themselves through years of work, study, and practice in order to "put it all together" in what seems to be a smooth, effortless, unselfconscious rhythm of play. The "natural" athlete cannot become professional and last in the big-time game unless his natural skills are focused, disciplined, practiced. To be good at anything requires commitment, effort, endurance, patience. Anyone who suggests differently simply doesn't understand what life is all about.

The trouble with the hedonists is not that they overestimate the importance of play; it is that they do not understand the dynamics or the phenomenology of play. They think that in a casual, transient relationship, without care or commitment, play can become possible. They don't believe that the skills, the discipline, the involvement that is required for success in all other games is somehow or other not required for success in the sexual game. The sexual player, according to the hedonist view, is dispensed from the existential obligations that are imposed on those who would play any other kind of game well. One can, they imply, quickly establish a rapport of easy, practiced, subtle communication with another partner that one has just met. One can engage in a complex, intricate sexual dance with someone to whom no commitment has been made and with whom no particular affection is shared. One can, in other words, play the sexual game according to an entirely different set of rules than are required for every other kind of game that humankind knows.

One can, of course, obtain sexual release from virtually any partner. One can experience a certain kind of thrill from conquering a new partner and from engaging in an illicit or forbidden relationship. But such satisfactions are neither very profound nor very durable and are peripheral to the sexual game. One also can find in casual, transient relationships a certain sort of variety (an argument used by the enthusiastic apostles of "swinging"). If "variety" means coupling with another body, and another and another, there can be no real "relationship" other than the old "slam, bang, thank you mam!" type. If "variety" means variation within the lovemaking, then the one- or two-time encounter provides little opportunity for experimentation and innovation. When two people make love for the first time they are both too deeply concerned with the impression they are making on the other and with their own pleasure and satisfaction to venture into the various forms of pleasure giving and taking. The subtle, sophisticated, implicit communication that makes for variety in human relationships simply does not have time to grow in a brief encounter. They meet, they mate, they separate; and not much else occurs. Playfulness and transiency are contradictory to one another. All the rich, elaborate mystery of another human being's body and spirit simply cannot be discovered except in a long-term relationship. Unless one begins to understand the mysteries of another's personhood, then playfulness and the variety which is the fruit of playfulness will not even begin to exist.

We display that which is consistently best in ourselves only in a context where we have some reassurance and security. If one's idea of sex is merely a routine coupling of bodies, then trust, security and commitment are unnecessary. But if one believes that sexual playfulness involves the sharing of that which is best in both body and spirit, one must inevitably conclude that time, patience, practice, and commitment are as absolutely essential for the sexual game as they are for any other.

You play with those you care about. You let others play with you only if you are reasonably persuaded that they care about you. This is not an option that one may exercise or not; it is part of the fundamental interpersonal dynamics of the human condition. Play without trust, without confidence, without care, without commitment simply will not persist—indeed it will not even begin. Perhaps the reason why so many of the apostles of contemporary hedonism seem so dreadfully dreary when they talk about play is because they are not very playful people and those relationships they extol are anything but playful. Hedonism may provide variety of a sort, but there is no opportunity to develop the practiced, disciplined interactions with another specific human being that is the absolutely indispensable prerequisite for successful play.

One does not have to make this point for any other game. No one in his right mind would expect the football player, the nightclub performer, the figure skater, the chess champion to be good without practice. No one would expect any member of a team to be instantaneously skillful at interacting with other members. The need for practice and skills is so obvious in most playful relationships that only a fool would deny it. Nonetheless, both the hedonist and the puritan seem to assume that humans are born with practiced skills in sexuality, skills which can easily and smoothly be invested in any relationship.

Most young people about to begin their lives together simply will not believe it when they are told that they know virtually nothing about what it takes to be a skilled sexual partner. Their world-view demands either that they possess total sexual competence at the very beginning of their relationship or that they acquire it almost instantaneously. The thought that it might take years for them to be skillful lovers—at least as many years as it takes a quarterback and a wide receiver to perfect their style with one another—is simply intolerable. After all, what else is there to the sexual game but manipulating a couple of organs and merging two bodies? What else is a playmate besides someone who can give you pleasure and to whom you can bring pleasure? Why should it be all that difficult?

Similarly those who have been together for a long time may be deeply affronted if it is suggested that they may still be sexual amateurs. Such a suggestion is taken as a nasty reflection of their competence as human beings, man or woman. It may well be, of course, that the greatest athletes are the old pros, people in their late thirties and early forties like George Blanda, Y. A. Tittle, Johnny Unitas, Sonny Jurgensen, and, awhile back, Bobby Lane. You may have to be thirty-five or forty to have acquired all the skills of a truly great quarterback. And it may not be all that much different for a lover. In fact, loving another human being makes quarterbacking look easy, and a couple committed to each other on a sustained basis should be coming into their prime skills as lovers in their middle years of life. That most people have long since become satisfied, if not complacent, with skills in lovemaking that have not developed at all may be evidence of many things but surely not that loving is easy. The complex psychological and physiological skills required for intimacy and for intimate playfulness must be learned throughout a lifetime. Whenever we think we have learned it all about loving another human being, then we have in fact retired from the game of love.

The requirement of sustained commitment is not imposed from the outside by a prescient deity who spends a good deal of his time devising ways to make the life of humans miserable. It is rather something that flows from the fundamental dynamic of human relationships. If you are satisfied with superficial, shallow, pedestrian sex, then you can take your pleasure wherever you find it and lead the playboy life of noninvolvement. If you want depth, richness, variety, and playfulness in your sexual expressions, there is simply no other way to have it than to acquire a partner and settle down to a long life of exploration, revelation, experimentation and growth, development, mistakes, learning, progress, effort, patience, practice, and perseverance. It is a very difficult affair (pun intended). It is a very high price to pay for playful sex, but there is no other way to acquire the commodity.

Sustained commitment does not automatically guarantee playfulness, of course. On the contrary, in many, many cases a sustained commitment of a sort coexists with dullness and monotony. Commitment does not guarantee playfulness; it is merely the absolutely essential precondition for it. One might wish that it were otherwise, but in fact it is not, and there is nothing much we can do about it.

Those who argue against permanency in the marriage commitment point out that such permanent commitments frequently are nothing more than a context for a life of mediocrity, exploitation, and frustration. I do not wish to debate the point that middle-class marriage in America is frequently frustrating, dull and exploitive, but it does not follow that more rewarding and challenging relationships can be found in the so-called "new" sexual forms (most of which, incidentally, are very old). What one calls a relationship is considerably less important than whether there is a sustained commitment to the perennial development of the skills required for human love. It is that kind of commitment and that kind of commitment *only* which can guarantee the growth of the knowledge, the understanding, the affection, the skill, the practiced ease, the disciplined resourcefulness, the creative and insightful spontaneity necessary for sexual playfulness. Anything less than that may not be a caricature of marriage but it is surely a form of human sexuality that is less than it might be. It is a shame when humans settle for something less than what might have been, especially when it might have been had with only a little more courage, a little more trust, a bit more willingness to take risks, a little bit more faith.

The obvious implication of the line of reasoning developed in this chapter is that sexual variety is much more likely to be found in the exploration of the depths and the possibilities of one relationship than in flitting from one shallow and transient encounter to another. The psychological validity of such an insight is, I think, unarguable. That many psychologists are reluctant to apply it to sexuality, while readily applying it to other forms of behavior, is evidence that the psychological profession is not always willing to follow its own insights, particularly when they seem to ally them with the traditional wisdom.

For some people, particularly the young, the important point is that playfulness can only be achieved in the context of a sustained commitment. For many others, particularly the not-so-young, the important point is that sexual playfulness can indeed be achieved in a marriage relationship, and that the relationship is never too old to be reborn. It is not necessary to sell the young on the possibility of love or a need for a variety within it, but the not-so-young have often made their peace with the absence of variety, think they can do without it, and may even be convinced that it is not possible to achieve. The ultimate conclusion of such existential pessimism is that variety probably is not a good thing after all.

It is precisely at that point that we must turn to our religious symbols. Is variety good? Is variety necessary? Is variety possible? Is there any room for diversity, excitement, novelty in the human condition?

The Christian response to the mystery of variety, plurality, diversity is the symbol of the Holy Spirit, that dimension of the Deity which represents creativity, spontaneity, diversity. If the principle of unity is the Father, the principle of multiplicity and diversity is the Spirit. The Spirit is a wheeling, dealing, whirling, twirling, dancing, darting poltergeist Deity, who flits and leaps, spins, and dives, dashes in madcap movement through the cosmos, flicking out sparks of creativity and vitality wherever he goes. (In Ireland I think the Holy Spirit becomes a leprechaun.) The Spirit is a howling, raging wind, blazing, leaping fire, passionate, protective dove. He blows where he will, stirs up what he wants, speaks to us with the howling of a hurricane or the gentle touch of an evening breeze in the summertime. He calls forth that which is best, most generous, most giving, most risk-taking in ourselves. He stirs us up out of complacency, mediocrity, monotony, routine. He is the Spirit of life, of vitality, of excitement, of adventure. He is the Spirit of play, and, together with the creative Word, he dances and sings and claps his hands, as God the Father produces his splendid, variegated, excessive—indeed half-mad—universe. It may even have been the Holy Spirit who poured the cups of the wine of love that intoxicated the creative Father to produce the wild, manic splendor of his creation. The sins against the Holy Spirit are those of despair, giving up, settling down and not seeking more.

Can one believe in this madcap, merry Spirit and still believe that playfulness is unimportant, unrequired, indeed impossible in human sexuality? One can, perhaps, but then one is not a Christian.

chapter 3

Part of the excitement of any game is its mystery.
One does not know how the game will end; indeed, one can't be absolutely certain what will
happen in the next moment. One may know the
"moves" of those one plays with, but yet, for all
the knowledge and skill one may have acquired
in playing the game, the others are still a source of
constant surprise. As the most intimate of games,
sex is also the most mysterious. One can live with
another human being for years and still not even
begin to plumb the mystery of that other person.
The more one knows about the other, the more
one discovers there is to be known. The very fact
that we discover something about the other and
bring that particular aspect of his mystery into

the open, the more his deeper mysteries begin to actuate themselves in his personality. The more we know them the more strange they become. Another human is either a closed and uninteresting book or a constant and endless source of fascination. Whether he be interesting or not depends as much on our definition of and response to him as on any intrinsic quality of his own nature.

Perhaps the greatest weakness in the preparation that young people receive today for marriage is that no one tells them that life together will be and ought to be an ongoing series of surprises, of discoveries made, of sudden and illuminating bursts of understanding and self-revelation. New puzzles, obscurities, and secrets will be ever-present to be probed, explored, and understood. Young people know that there is pleasure and fascination in discovering the body of the other and permitting one's own body to be discovered by the other, but that part of the mystery of revelation and self-discourse is relatively uncomplex. A man may indeed go through decades of married life and understand very little of either the physiology of female sexuality or that of his wife. Still, learning what gives a woman pleasure and what in particular is pleasure to *his* woman is relatively simple compared to the understanding of the deeper mystery of the human personality that creates the context of his wife's sexuality and which is focused so sharply in the ambience of their sexual encounters. Similarly, the woman may not be particularly interested in discovering what really turns her husband on, but after a while she avoids knowledge on the subject only at considerable effort. The mystery of who and what her man is in the depths of his soul, however, is one about which she can remain serenely unaware throughout the duration of her marriage.

As an absolutely indispensable prerequisite, then, for sexual playfulness, a man and a woman must be determined to get to know one another, which means that they must be determined to commit themselves to endless exploration of the heights and depths and breadths of the mysteries of each other's selfhood. We can only understand another person's sex when we can grasp it in the context of the totality of who and what he is, and that is a lifelong challenge. The more we know the other person, the more influence we have over him. The more we permit the other to know us, the more influence we surrender to him. The greater our knowledge of the other, the more erotic our relationship will become. The process of exploring another's personality is extremely erotic, much more so, in fact, than exploring the other's body, though the two processes go on simultaneously, heightening and reenforcing the pleasurability of both. It is relatively easy, it turns out, to live with a stranger, but we cannot play well with one, no more than can a quarterback and a wide receiver who do not know each other. If one wishes to have playful sex, then one must accept the burden of endless exploration, but one should also understand that after a while the exploration becomes more than a burden and a challenge, an adventure and reward in itself. To explore the depths of someone else's personality is the most erotic thing a human being can do, and when that exploration is reinforced and facilitated by sexual lovemaking, the lovemaking becomes an episode in a grand adventure, taking on an intensity of pleasure that it would otherwise not have. There are, of course, costs incurred in the acquisition of intimate knowledge and influence over another. The heaviest cost is that one permits the other to have knowledge of and influence over oneself. In addition, time, that most precious commodity in our busy society, is required, as is patience, tact, taste, and courage. It is much, much easier to buy a copy of *Playboy* or advertise in one of the spouse-swapping journals.

From the secure perspective provided only to the celibate outsider, I am always amused by how confident husbands and wives are that they understand their spouses perfectly when it is quite clear, even to the most casual observer, that they understand little if anything about their partner. Somehow or other it is a sign of failure, of inadequacy, of ineptitude to admit that the spouse is a mystery that one is only beginning dimly to understand. In truth, such an admission is a sign of the beginning of wisdom.

After a number of years together there are some things we do know about our spouses: what kind of food they like, what their musical tastes are, what kind of drinks they are likely to order, what kind of mood they are likely to be in in the mornings, how they respond to sickness, inconvenience, stress. This capacity to predict some of their responses lulls us into the complacent conviction that we know everything there is to be known, we understand everything that is to be understood. Of course, the other party may know some things about us, but he is remarkably unperceptive and really doesn't understand us at all; we understand him, though. Oddly enough, he feels exactly the same way.

There is a substantial difference between knowing some things about another human being and *knowing* that other human being. Each one of us is aware of how complex, intricate, and baffling we are even to ourselves. Anyone with even a small capacity for self-examination knows that he is a bundle of mysteries, enigmas, and contradictions, but somehow it is difficult to face making the leap from accepting our own complexities and mystery to realizing that everyone else is as baffling as we are. "My husband is an open book; I am a mystery." "My wife is transparent; I am an enigma." It is a totally unreasonable position, but still a useful one that we are most reluctant to give up.

A young man takes unto himself a wife. He acquires a traveling companion, a housekeeper, a sexual partner, a joint administrator, a potential parent. Her body is delightful to hold, a joy to possess even though he is awkward and uncomfortable in their early attempts at sexual union, and she is neither as responsive nor seductive as her warmth and affection before marriage suggested she would be. Still, they work out some sort of minimal level of sexual adjustment and settle down for their life together. He discovers that she is not quite the person he thought she was when he decided that he should marry her. She can be moody, unpredictable, sometimes very unreasonable. They get along well enough together, and there are satisfactions and rewards as they build a common life and begin to raise their children. They quarrel and fight, make up and love, and slowly develop a long agenda of frustrations and anger and hurt that they cannot or will not discuss. She is a good wife—not quite the kind he had expected but better than most. In any event, he understands her, knows what is necessary to keep her happy, and what must be done to reduce the strains and tensions in their joint life to a reasonable minimum. What more, after all, can be expected in this very imperfect world we live in.

And yet he has married a stranger; he lives with a stranger (and she does too). No one ever told him that a spouse was a mystery and that one must devote considerable time and effort to probing the recesses of that mystery. His wife is much like all other women, although in many ways she is quite unique and special. He must value and appreciate her specialness, and he understands her and is able to keep her in line by yielding on the things he must yield on and partly by insisting on the things he knows she will yield. The gene combination that produced her physiology is a combination that never existed before and will never exist again. She comes to marriage with a personality, a value system, and a series of interpretive schemes, a fantasy life, a collection of longings, hungers, fears, anxieties that are totally her own. Her social class, her ethnic groups, her religion, the places she grew up in—country, region, neighborhood—the kinds of friends she had, the schools she went to, her adolescent sexual experiences, her relationships with her mother, father, siblings—all of these, combined with the major cultural events of her adolescence and youth and the genetic code of her biological being, produced a complex, delicate, mysterious, fascinating woman who is reduced to a series of propositions and predictions only at the risk of devastating misunderstanding. A husband may be able to sort out and organize some of the more obvious characteristics and behavior, but because he knows how she is likely to respond in given sets of stimuli, it does not follow that he has the foggiest notion of why she so responds—and she may not herself.

She has shared her body with him and a good part of her life space; she has also shared some of her more obvious moods, fears, hopes, and dreams. But there are vast areas of her selfhood which are still intensely private and which she does not want to share or does not know how to share or could not share. It is not necessary for him to know everything about her; there are some things that he need not know, other things he should not know, and still others he will never know. None of this really matters, though. What counts is that if they are to be playmates there is a good deal more that he can and must know. Sometime during the course of their marriage the husband must decide that his wife is an open book, pleasant enough to live with, but containing few mysteries and challenges; or he must decide that she is endlessly fascinating and he will devote the rest of his life to her in pleasured fascination. He will encourage her mystery and her uniqueness, because by permitting her to live more fully the mystery she is, he is freeing her to be an enticing, seductive, pliable, playful, aggressive, demanding, yielding lover. And he can stop the pretense of *knowing* her, which is so stilting and limiting to her, him, and their life together.

The decision-point of the husband's making up his mind whether his wife is a mystery or a transparency is of critical importance for their marriage. It is, of course, a decision that can be reversed. He may discover to his chagrin that her mystery and uniqueness do not indeed fascinate him, and he may have to make another decision to go back to the more placid plateau of unquestioning coexistence in order to keep the family together. To retreat from intimacy is tragic, but to deny that it may be necessary or a decision consciously taken is to refuse to admit the complexity and difficulty of interpersonal relationships. "Getting to Know You," as the song from *The King and I* avers, is great fun; still, many husbands and wives think that that period is far behind them in their life together. Perhaps it is, but when the period of getting to know someone is over, the period of playfulness is over too.

Janet and Lawrence had been married fifteen years. All their friends thought it was a happy marriage. They were a handsome couple; they had two cars, a beautiful home, apparently all the money they needed. Their three children were attractive and well behaved. Janet was perhaps a bit too compulsive about her family responsibilities; Lawrence was maybe a little over-committed to his career as an architect. She might have been better off if she got out of the house more; he might have been better off if he were in it more. Still, compared to most of their friends, they seemed to have an ideal marital adjustment.

And then suddenly Janet walked out. She was tired of Lawrence and wanted a life of her own. There was no other man, really, although she was close to having an affair with a divorced friend of theirs. She didn't hate Lawrence and still loved their children, but life with him had become intolerably dull and boring. She wanted to begin to live again.

As the two of them talked, it became clear that they were total strangers. Two years of dating, a year of engagement, and fifteen years of marriage; yet they knew almost nothing about one another. They were strangers who shared the same house, the same children, and sometimes the same bed (though not that very often anymore). But they knew less about each other than Lawrence knew about some of his professional colleagues and Janet did about some of her friends in their town. Their relationship had deteriorated into nonexistence.

Lawrence had always been fiercely competitive in everything he did. On the athletic field, in school, in his work he was driven to excel. He wanted to be the very best, because his father, whom he adored, had been the very best. His competitiveness was not abnormal but it was very strong. He saw in Janet a warm, witty, charming young woman who would create for him an atmosphere of graciousness and sophistication as respite from the battles of the professional world. Janet had a weak father and an overpowering mother. She saw in Lawrence a strong, competent male who would free her from the need to worry compulsively about "responsibilities," which her mother had drummed into her. It seemed like a perfect match.

It was and it wasn't. There were aspects of Lawrence's personality—his strength, his drive, his assertiveness—which Janet desperately needed. And there were aspects of her personality—laughter, elegance, intelligence—that he needed. But unfortunately they rarely saw these dimensions of one another. For all his competitiveness, Lawrence was afraid of women (just as his father had been). He didn't know how to be anything but diffident when he encountered resistance or opposition from a woman. Janet's network of compulsive responsibilities—she spent weeks working on a Christmas card list each year—was designed to compensate for the guilt she felt over the powerful, passionate drives she had to work so hard to control.

Janet had not the slightest idea that her husband was afraid of women, and especially of her. In fact, when she was told she could not believe it —even though everyone else who knew Lawrence could see his fear after about five minutes. Similarly, Lawrence had no notion of the wild furies of anger, hatred, love, and ambition that stirred in his wife's soul. When he was around she seemed to be dull and pale, though he would quickly add that she was a fine mother and did a great job with the children. Everyone else knew that she was part witch and part bitch—the sexiest woman on the street. But the flare and the fire which she displayed at their dinner parties quickly died when the guests left, and she became the dumpy house-wife her husband had always taken for granted.

Their sex life mirrored the rest of their relationship. Janet hated herself for it, but she entered marriage a prude, ashamed of her body and terrified at the thought of intercourse. She was not exactly frigid in bed, but she was almost totally passive. A coquette at cocktail parties, she became shy and embarrassed in the bedroom. Even after a decade-and-a-half of marriage she found it almost impossible to undress in the presence of a man. Her body, supremely graceful when she walked down the street, became awkward and ungainly as soon as it lost the protection of clothes. She assented to intercourse whenever she was asked, but her lack of enthusiasm was obvious.

Lawrence had absorbed from his family environment the belief that the fears and anxieties of a woman should be deferred to always. His wife turned out to be a weak, frightened woman. She wasn't the kind of person he thought he had married, but he was still responsible for her. He would protect her and humor her peculiarities. He "lost interest" in sex because, as he put it, it didn't seem fair that he should be the only one enjoying it. He would not admit it to himself, but he was terrified at the thought of what might happen if he tried to force beyond his wife's compulsiveness and prudery. So he lost himself in his work and the success it brought him. He thought of his family as a successful joint venture in child-rearing.

It was a nice arrangement. There were no risks on either side, or so it seemed. Neither party got what they had expected originally in sex or inter-personal support, but the adjustment, while at a low level of payoff, seemed to work. They had mutual interests in art and music, friends, their house, their social life, their children. It was fool-ish to expect anything more from marriage.

They still had hazy memories of the dreams of each other's strength they had when they entered marriage, and each still had sexual fantasies. There were times, at night after a party, perhaps, when Lawrence would have a powerful fantasy of ripping the clothes from Janet's body, spending the rest of the night in a wild sexual orgy com-posed of all manner of unspeakable things. He quickly dismissed such images as adolescent fool-ishness; still, he would have liked to be able to be an adolescent fool with his wife. Part of his fan-tasy was that midway through the orgy she would turn on him, take the sexual initiative and over-whelm him. There was never any danger of some-thing like that happening in the real world.

But Janet's fantasies were remarkably similar —though they did not involve her husband. She was ashamed of it, but the image of a strong, over-powering man raping her were frequent and com-pellingly vivid. Her imagination lingered on every tiny detail of the assault. While the rape was never cruel, it was always a violent sexual experience that forced her out of her shame and turned her into a passionate respondent first and then into an aggressor, matching violence with violence. Furthermore, despite her prudery (probably because of it), she had strong exhibitionist fantasies of being stripped and exposed, fantasies which were as delightful as they were terrifying. In both fantasies, of course, her doubts about her own worth and attractiveness as a woman were removed by the forceful actions of others, the kind of actions that were completely absent in her marriage. Unlike Lawrence, she was unable to lose her frustrations in work. Her moving out was an act of desperation.

Janet's and Lawrence's fantasies, then, were as potentially complementary as was everything else about their personalities. Each had chosen the right partner in marriage on solid intuitive if not explicit grounds. But a pattern had developed in their relationship which, instead of playing to each other's strengths, reinforced their weaknesses. They were bringing out in each other exactly the opposite of what both of them needed and suppressing exactly what was needed.

There were psychological reasons for such a vicious circle. Therapy may well be an important part of any rehabilitation of their marriage, but neither Lawrence nor Janet was particularly neurotic. Their personality problems certainly helped them in their implicit conspiracy to live together as strangers for fifteen years. But if they are to salvage anything of their life together, they must begin to get to know one another. Fifteen years late is better than never.

Janet was a beautiful, intelligent, complex, challenging woman. To explore the subtleties of her body and spirit would have looked to many men like the opportunity of a lifetime and an opportunity for a lifetime. Her husband didn't see any mystery at all. Lawrence was the kind of vigorous, dynamic, active male that many women find irresistibly fascinating. If he had wanted to be unfaithful it would have been easy. Janet fled him because he was utterly and unbearably dull.

Because they did not know one another they had no influence over one another. Without influence there can be no possibility of growth within a relationship. By "influence" I mean the ability to obtain desired behavior from another human being. The word has taken on bad connotations in our society, but it is impossible for there to be any close human relationship without influence. By the very fact that we love someone he or she has influence over us. And by the very fact that we are loved we have influence over the one who loves us. Influence in intimate relationships can be bad or good; it is good when used to promote the growth of the best dimensions of another's personality and bad when it is used to manipulate and constrain him. We all know how to get something from those who are close to us. We nag or sulk or have a temper tantrum. We know that the other will cave in when we use certain techniques to obtain a desired result. Neither person grows in such an exchange, but in many intimate relationships it is the only use of influence known.

There is another kind of influence that goes far beyond manipulation. It is based on a knowledge of the other person that goes much deeper than knowing what kind of pressure will force him to cave in and do what we want. Such knowledge comes from a serious and sustained exploration of the depths of the other's self. When we have this knowledge we have immense power over the other—to hurt him, indeed, but also to free him. With our knowledge we become skilled at creating an environment in which the other is almost certain to respond the way we want—and the way that the best in him wants.

Janet wanted a lover who would break through her compulsions, fears, guilts, and prudery so that she could give free rein to her wild, creative, passionate personality. She married Lawrence because she sensed—perhaps not in so many words—that he was such a man. It seemed to her that she had made a mistake. In fact she had not. He had the capabilities to be such a husband. If she had gotten to know him she would have discovered his fear of women and also his longings to be the passionate lover she wanted. If she had studied his behavior, his responses, his cues, she would have been able to devise a strategy that would virtually compel him to break through his fears. It would not have been merely a matter of encouraging him but of understanding his fear of women and systematically demolishing that fear.

Similarly, if Lawrence had realized how much his wife wanted to be free of her compulsions and sexual passivity, he would have perceived that a strategy of refusing to tolerate her endless hours of worrying over Christmas card lists might have freed her. Instead of accepting her compulsions he should have simply demanded that they stop. She would have responded quickly and even gratefully. Furthermore, he could have swept aside her prudery and insisted on undressing her himself every night instead of letting her sneak away to the bathroom to change. She might have resisted in terror at first—but not for very long —since the delights from such rough treatment would have been too great.

It was not ill will or neurosis (though there was some of both in their relationship) that kept them from dealing effectively with one another. It was ignorance, an ignorance which was totally un-necessary.

But why do we know so little about those who are close to us? There are three reasons, I think. First, it never occurs to us that we are living in a house with a mystery that can be a source of end-less fascination and enjoyment. We think that we know all there is to know of the other and simply stop learning more. After you have been married ten years, what is there left to learn? The answer is that there is an immense amount to learn, but most people simply won't believe it.

Second, we are too busy thinking about ourselves and worrying about what the other is thinking about us to try to figure out what is going on inside him or her. Janet was disgusted with herself, frustrated with her marriage, disappointed with Lawrence, and guilty for having failed him. But in all of these emotions (and in the comparable ones in Lawrence) there is not the slightest hint of curiosity about the fears, the dreams, the expectations, the disappointments, the hopes of the other. If Janet had turned her attention away from her own failures and from Lawrence's inadequacies to wonder about the real Lawrence, she might have discovered his fear of women. In the process she would have taken her mind off herself and might have begun to see the possibility of excitement in their relationship. But Lawrence had long since stopped being a mystery and had become merely part of the scenery, to be accepted unchanged, unchanging, and unchangeable.

Finally, to explore the mystery of another human is work, and we are lazy. It is also risk, because we must reveal ourselves in the process of constraining another to reveal himself. If Lawrence had worked up enough energy to probe into the subtle complexities of his wife's sexual fears and longings, he inevitably would have revealed much about his own sexuality in the process. It would have been a delightful interchange but also dangerous. No telling where things might have gone—though probably not to the divorce court.

But how do we get to know someone else? Let's suppose we acknowledge that we live with strangers. How do we break through the strangeness?

First of all, we pay attention to what we already know but have not bothered to interpret. Lawrence knew—and resented—the kind of men Janet seemed to enjoy. He knew the sort of person she was likely to spar with in her bright, witty chatter. They were men like himself. When Janet was not around he could behave that way with other women. Such exchanges may not be seriously intended but they are of course filled with sexual overtones, invitations, and responses. If Janet liked to flirt with tough, aggressive, demanding men, and if he could be that way, then maybe his gentle diffidence in the face of her passivity was the result of a complete misreading of the situation. He had all the facts, he simply hadn't put them together and interpreted them.

Second, we learn from cues that have been there all along but which we have missed. There are aspects of the mystery of our intimate stranger that are easy to see but we have not noticed. Janet knew that her husband was a hard-driving professional with almost limitless ambition, but around her he was dull and uninteresting. She was torn between thinking that he was undersexed and that she was unattractive. But if she had been at all curious about probing into the mystery that was her husband she would have noticed rather quickly that he tended to be very quiet when meeting a woman for the first time. "Why, Lawrence is shy!" she might exclaim in disbelief. "He's afraid of women!" And it would dawn on her, "Good heavens, he's afraid of *me!*" There are no easy ways out of any human problem, but if Janet had come upon this insight early in their marriage she might have had an exciting and enjoyable time leading this man away from his fears of women while capturing him completely in her femininity. Changing the focus from "What's wrong with him?" and "What's wrong with me?" to "What can I do for him?" might have effected a major transformation in their relationship. The facts were all there; she simply hadn't looked at them.

Finally, we must probe beyond the facts about the intimate stranger to get at the real person. There are times and places when people talk about themselves, sometimes in response to our questions, more likely in response to our interest and affection. Janet knew that Sunday breakfast was one of the few times in the week when Lawrence liked to relax, expand, and talk about himself, his work, his plans. She did her best to cut such sessions short because Sunday was one of those days when her schedule of "ought-to-be-doing" was particularly long. But it was during that half-hour on Sunday morning that Lawrence was most open, most vulnerable, most easy to probe and explore. The trouble was that she didn't think there was anything to explore. Instead of guaranteeing privacy for that half-hour in which she could snuggle up to him with affection, she would wait impatiently, car keys in hand, for the session to end so that she could get on to the important things.

Janet was most likely to be expansive at the end of the evening over a second drink after the TV news. Since Lawrence had given up using such occasions as a prelude to sex (not that he ever tried very hard), he turned on Johnny Carson and became absorbed in the screen while his wife made seemingly pointless and inane comments about herself. If he thought there was any mystery at all left in this intimate stranger, he would have turned off the TV, put his arm around his wife, listened very carefully to what she said, and discovered a very different woman from the one he thought he was married to.

It all sounds very calculating. Our current cult of spontaneity has led us to believe that such careful, systematic, even devious exploration of the personality of another is dishonest and even immoral. The loud, aggressive, frequently punitive behavior of the encounter group is supposed to be virtuous, and the persistent, gentle, indirect probing of the intimate stranger is thought to be wrong. Still, all the encounter sessions in the world could not cure what is wrong with the marriage of Janet and Lawrence. An encounter session might reveal to them that they are strangers; it could never make them friends.

What will become of them? I would like to be able to say that their problems were solved, but I cannot. All that I can say is that they have begun to see the problems and are trying, indeed trying very hard. That is all that can be asked of anyone. Janet and Lawrence—like most of us—will have to keep trying for the rest of their lives.

Playfulness may seem to be so heavy a burden, so complex a responsibility, so difficult a task that we might be tempted to give it up and settle for routine mediocrity, which if it is not much fun is not nearly so demanding. Life is hard enough without adding more mystery to it. If one has to work so hard in order to be playful, maybe play isn't worth the effort.

But in fact, probing the mystery of another human being is not preparation for the game, it is the game itself. Getting to know someone is not merely a prelude to eroticism, it is vividly erotic in itself. One gets to know another human being not by serious, sober, dour, and unimaginative cross-examination but by playing with the person. It is in times of fantasy and festivity, merriment and frolic, that another person is most likely to reveal himself. Precisely at those times the guards, the defenses, the masks are most likely to be down. We do not force the mysteries and the secrets out of another human being; we seduce them out by attention, affection, encouragement, reassurance, and laughter. To tease slowly the body of the spouse from indifference to a height of passionate desire is as erotic, if not more so, than the culmination of the teasing process in orgasm. Or to put it more precisely, sexual satisfaction that comes at the end of a slow, gentle, seductive prelude is infinitely more satisfying than one that is quickly, hastily, and urgently experienced. An analogous process is at work in probing the mysteries of the other's personality in which sexuality is necessarily a critical dimension but not the only one. We explore the other's personality as we explore her sexuality—slowly, gently, encouragingly. The technique of seduction persuades her to share ever more of her endlessly fascinating selfhood with us. It is work, perhaps, but it is delightful, enjoyable, and playful work.

Our friends Janet and Lawrence might be appalled at the thought that after fifteen years they must begin over again almost as perfect strangers. Worse than that, they must begin as strangers with a long agenda of frustration and shared antagonisms. Still, they might look at it differently. Lawrence might consider that much to his surprise, he is living with a mysterious, fascinating stranger, one whom it would be a great pleasure to get to know. He must begin again, or begin for the first time, to discover what her sexual needs, pleasures, and fantasies are. But while he is learning about her sexually he must at the same time begin to get to know who she is. This, too, can be a pleasure so overwhelming that it can transform his whole life. Furthermore, the fact that all of this is in some fashion a way of making up for and reversing past failures can make the experience even more rewarding.

Janet, for her part, could make the same assumptions and embark upon the same pleasurable adventure of winning for herself this attractive stranger who lives in the same house with her. For both of them, of course, the critical decision is to redefine each other from being an open book to being a fascinating stranger. This is not easy to do at the beginning of a marriage and much less so after many years have passed. But it is still possible, and when the spouse becomes an intimate, mysterious stranger, an enticing, irresistibly attractive stranger, the stage is set for sexual play to begin. The players may begin as amateurs, but so long as they realize that there is much to learn, there is no reason why they should not eventually become professionals.

Those of us who were raised in a rationalist Cartesian world, in which science confidently expected to be able to explain everything, manipulate everything, solve everything, do not like mysteries. They are an affront to our rationality and to our Enlightenment optimism. Religiously a mystery was something that had to be believed under pain of mortal sin, that undigested lump of religious truth for which we could not give a rational defense. We read mystery stories because we expect solutions at the end. A mystery then is either a puzzle to be solved or an obscure doctrine to be swallowed. Scientific philosophers (more frequently than scientists themselves) confidently predicted that soon there would be no mysteries left, and theologians like Rudolf Bultmann said that it was impossible to see mystery in a bolt of electricity across the sky when we could control electricity with a flick of a light switch. When we hear that sex is mysterious, that our sexual partner is a mystery, and that sex cannot be playful unless we recognize its mysteriousness, we are affronted. Sex is, after all, a biological function. Skill can be acquired by learning certain bits of biological information. Sexual hang-ups are the result of either childhood experience or oppressive social structure or old-fashioned religious dogmas. It is an ordinary biological function; how can it possibly be a mystery?

But the younger generation is fascinated by mystery. It realizes that science cannot explain everything, and the best scientists no longer purport to do so. The cosmos is not a machine to be understood and manipulated but a mystery to be explored. Astrology, the I Ching, folklore, occult wisdom are all to be explored, because they might reveal hints and secrets about the meaning of life and about how humans ought to live. As Father Charles Meyer points out in his brilliant book, *Man of God* (Doubleday, 1970), we are now moving from the mystagogic to the mystadylic era;

that is to say, from a time when we explained mysteries away as puzzles to be solved to a time when we explore mysteries for the secrets to be found there. Sex, like everything else in the world, is indeed ordinary and commonplace; but it shares intimately in the fundamental mysteries of the universe. Why is there anything at all? Why is there a struggle between good and evil? Why is there both unity and diversity? He who thinks that sex is only mystery blinds himself to the ordinariness of human life, but he who thinks that it is only biology blinds himself to the mystery that pervades the cosmos. Mysteries, as any addict of Nero Wolfe, Agatha Christie, Ngaio Marsh, and Ross McDonald knows, are fun. And the greatest mystery of all, the mystery of why I am and where I am going, ought to be the greatest fun of all. The passion, power, the pleasure, the pain of sexual intimacy is deeply involved in ways we only dimly perceive with that agonizing question. As we find that other who is our love, we also find ourselves, and in the process the two of us may begin to find the Other who is our Lover.

In the mystagogic world mysteries are sacraments, revelations of great secrets, and not so much obscure puzzles as dazzling rays of light. Sex, then, is mystery, sacrament, revelation. To discover who our lover and ourself really are is to discover something fundamental about the cosmos.

Or as St. Paul says, sexual union is a great sacrament, a great *mysterion*, which reveals the intimacy of God's union with his creatures. We may be content to write off our sex life as a prosaic, pedestrian, biological function. When we do that we miss something the great mystics and the great lovers, the great poets and the great visionaries down through the ages have perceived. When a man and woman are locked in an embrace they come for a few brief seconds close to the core of the greatest Mystery of them all.

chapter 4

The *Playboy* centerfold is an erotic picture, crudely, grossly erotic, and appeals primarily to adolescent sexual fantasies. The larger the body organs, the more sexual pleasure is promised. By her smile, her deportment, her casual invitation, the Playmate of the Month promises a fun-filled romp. No hang-ups, no involvements, no commitments, no furniture to buy, no risk of being tied down, no extra responsibilities—just fun and games now, as soon as you want, however you want it, whenever you want it. Images of play are there for the asking; one just has to plunk down a dollar. (If you are a woman, you have now achieved the marvelous equality of being able to plunk down your dollar for a copy of *Playgirl*.)

Let us leave aside the traditional concern over whether the *Playboy* centerfold is a "dirty" picture. (My own guess is that there are things to be found on the walls of the Vatican Museum and the ceiling of the Sistine Chapel that are more erotic.) Whatever the deficiencies the centerfolds of *Playboy* and *Playgirl* may have as part of the ancient tradition of erotic art, one must still observe that the play they promise is phony. First, the buxom young woman is not in fact prepared to play with anyone. She is posing for a picture for money and the considerable amount of fame and attention it will bring. She is not prepared to play with the cameraman taking her picture or the *Playboy* buyer who stares at her goggle-eyed. The invitation in her eyes, her smile, and the arrangement of her body may be an invitation to fantasy, but it is not in fact anything but an invitation to look. Looking may be fun, but it's not all that much fun. The *Playboy* philosophy, in fact, considers sex to be a spectator sport where participation is fantasy. The pro football fan not only admires Fran Tarkenton's ability to throw a pass, but he also identifies with him on the field. In fantasy he leaves his seat in front of the TV and descends to the gridiron and the battle being played out there. Similarly, the sexual spectator projects himself into the scene depicted in the centerfold and becomes involved in the actual game of sex to which the Playmate of the Month is inviting him.

A spectator sport may be diverting, but it is no substitute for the excitement of the real thing. It is also—and this is the point—much easier than the real thing. One can fantasize that one is Fran Tarkenton and still be woefully out of shape physically and unwilling to accept the pain or the possibility of losing. Every fan in the grandstand can be a great quarterback in dream life and it requires no discipline, no practice, no suffering at all. Similarly, one can play with the Playmate of the centerfold without ever having to practice or suffer the pain and discipline of acquiring skill as an effective player in the sexual game.

All the Playmate has to do is pose and smile. When one has overcome the embarrassment of it, it is a relatively easy task. There is no need to master the skills that the pose and smile imply. The Playmate of the Month looks playful, but in the real world she could be frigid, uninterested in men, terrified of sex, bitchy, or just plain blah in bed. The tease, the pose, the smile of the Playmate may be great for the reader's fantasy life and it may even make some marginal contribution to her own, but it has little relevance for anybody's sex life. It's not the phoniness that bothers us so much—that, after all, is an element in fantasy which concerns itself with the unreal, the puffed up, the make-believe. It is the pretense that this is what play is all about that rings so false.

To be a playmate or to have a playmate is at

least as difficult in its own order as being a professional quarterback. There are people who *look* like quarterbacks (and the Chicago Bears usually recruit them), but they haven't got what it takes. Strong arms, strong legs they may possess; and with the uniform and equipment they look great on the sports pages. But when the chips are down, it is the old bald men like Y. A. Tittle, grey-haired men like George Blanda, overweight men like Sunny Jurgensen and Bobby Lane, or sore-armed bandits like Johnny Unitas and John Haidel, or thin washed-out characters like Fran Tarkenton who score the final touchdown. It is not enough to look like a quarterback; one must be one. It is not enough to look like a Playmate; one must be good at playing.

To have a playmate means to be in possession of someone who has made themselves a specialist in your physiology-psychology-fantasy life. It means that you belong to someone who has devoted long years and much practice to understanding you and reading you and is perfectly happy continuing to practice and perfect his skills. It means that you have yielded yourself to the other's power and influence. To permit someone else to be your playmate is a delightful yet terrifying experience. As Martin D'Arcy pointed out long ago, love is not so much possessing as being possessed. Only the brave can permit themselves to be possessed. Your partner becomes the playmate when you have become brave enough to permit that partner to possess you. And when this happens there is no way out of the commitment. The question of the permanency of commitment becomes theoretical and irrevelant. When the kind of possession required for sexual playfulness has occurred, there is no way out; one does not want to get out, and even the thought of it is absurd. There may still be conflict and tension in the relationship; indeed, any relationship between humans will certainly generate some conflict. But being possessed by a playmate also means being obsessed by him (or her). As one young married man put it, "Murder? Yes! Divorce? Don't be silly!"

Sexual playfulness, then, begins in earnest only when one has given oneself to another so totally that there is simply no way back. In the fantasy of playing with the centerfold sex object the emphasis is almost always on what the spectator does to and with the body so invitingly displayed on the foldout. In real life, playfulness means what one is willing to permit the other to do to oneself. The male who indulges in his late adolescent fantasies with Playmate of the Month might very well be paralyzed with terror if the woman whose picture attracts him should stride into his real life and demand the kind of influence, power, and control over him that real life playmates must have if the game is to begin.

Similarly, the modern liberated woman who joins the growing ranks of those who buy *Playgirl* may shiver with anticipation at the fantasies which arise from the promises of the magazine. But in real life she is most reluctant to yield as much of herself to a man as would be required to make those fantasies anything but daydreams. A man as strong and as demanding and as resourceful and as persistent as the one in the centerfold would scare the living daylights out of her.

Real playmates are scary people, because they want us body and soul. If we give ourselves to them they will indeed provide all the pleasure and happiness they promise, but there will be fear and suffering in the constant struggle to become more fully possessed and to more fully possess. The centerfold characters—male or female—promise everything and demand nothing. Real playmates demand everything, and they are not satisfied until they get it. They learn only slowly and with difficulty how to effectively demand everything from us; and we learn only slowly and with difficulty how to respond to their demands. Both the playmate and the one with whom he (or she) plays acquire the skills of the game only with effort after mistakes, miscues, false starts, and failures.

Having a playmate and being one are reciprocal phenomena. Another person will be a playmate for us to the extent that we are fierce and determined enough to take possession of the other even as he (or she) is possessing us. We must be a specialist in the other's physiology-psychology-fantasy in the same way the other is a specialist in ours. There are no short cuts, no easy way out, no manuals to explain how to do it, no weekend courses to give us a degree validating our sexual playfulness. A good deal of the coin of the realm can be accumulated by those who write books and run weekend sessions on sex. There is titillation in them and the satisfaction that comes from feeling one is enlightened and a member of the avant garde—so perhaps those who read and attend get their money's worth. To give the sex manuals and the encounter movement the most I will concede to them, a little bit may happen to those involved in them in a few cases. But, in general, attempts to short circuit the long, slow difficult road to possession and being possessed may be fun but they are fundamentally counterfeit. They frequently reinforce the fears, the anxiety, the game-playing, the hiding behind masks that enable so many couples to escape the terrors of playing in the sexual game.

One of the principal obstacles to sexual play is the myth of competence. The assumption of the "Playboy Philosophy" and of more sophisticated forms of contemporary hedonism is that the spectator is already competent. Show a man the Playmate of the Month and he knows what to do to her; show a woman the centerfold of *Playgirl* and she knows how to react. Indeed, *Playboy* (and to a lesser and derivative extent, *Playgirl*, too) constantly flatters their readers by assuring them of their indubitable, unquestioned sexual omnicompetence. It's nice to be told we're good in bed, because we know we should be but have the sinking feeling that we are not.

Most adults know how babies are born. They know how sexual organs are made to be linked, and under appropriate circumstances they can perform the indicated operation with a certain minimum amount of efficiency. If that were all that is required to be an effective lover, then almost everyone would be sexually competent. Fears of sexual inadequacy that assail most of us would have no meaning at all.

But sex is between people, not merely between bodies. People are different; one can reach orgasm with a prostitute, but one can only play with another human whom he knows. And that brings us up against the mystery of another person's self.

Lock a man in a room with a Playmate of the Month and tell him he must make love to her. He will be sexually aroused, of course, but he will also be terrified because now he faces a real woman—attractive, mysterious, complex, baffling, able to respond at the promptings of herself, not only *his* fantasies. He can force himself crudely and brutally upon her and achieve the basic release that comes from orgasm; but this is not what his masculine ego and self-confidence demand of him. The interlude with this beautiful woman must be an event to remember, not just a few quick physiological spasms. She must enjoy it as much as he does. The totality of both their persons must be involved in a memorable and thoroughly satisfying experience. She is waiting for him to begin. What does she want? How should he start? How should they do it? How long should they prepare? What kind of foreplay would be best? What will really turn her on? What kinds of tenderness and affection will be most reassuring and stimulating? What can he do to make her respect and admire him? How can it be the kind of event that will make her want more of the same? How can he impress her as a sexually imaginative, creative, competent male? It is as though he has been put in the huddle of the Minnesota Vikings and called upon to deliver the game-winning pass when he can't even remember the game plan. Under such circumstances not a few men would become impotent and many others would simply turn into brutes. They are put into a situation where sexual competence is demanded of them immediately, and they simply do not know what to do.

Put a woman in the same situation where she is imprisoned with an extraordinarily attractive male who makes it perfectly clear that he is willing to make love. In her fantasy life she had dreamed repeatedly of having such a splendid male body available, but now she simply does not know what to do. Does he really find her attractive? Is she too thin or too fat? Are her sex organs too big or too small? Can she really hold his attention and interest? What should they talk about? How should she begin? What should she do with her hands and her mouth? What kinds of things would he like to do to her? Why is she so frightened? Is she frigid?

The point is, of course, that no matter how attractive we are we feel incompetent with strangers. It may be possible to do the bare minimum, although a man frightened into impotency by a strange encounter may not be able to do even that. Sexual competency is not a generalized ability, save for a few simple and easily learned physiological movements. It is an interpersonal competency gained with this particular person who happens to be our sexual partner at this particular segment of the space-time continuum. The stranger can't be a playmate because he (or she) doesn't know us and we don't know him. An interlude with a stranger may be successful enough to achieve mutual orgasmic release, and there may be a lucky occasion or two when strangers discover important physiological characteristics about one another quickly enough to heighten the pleasure of the experience. But the payoff declines rapidly, because there is far more in sexual play than the tension release of orgasm, however spectacular it may be. The strangers may become playmates, but they do so by exactly the same long, slow process of discovering the totality of one another's selfhood that occurs in any sustained sexual commitment. There is no reason, in other words, why this particular man and this particular woman should expect immediate sexual competency with one another. On the contrary, if they are wise they will expect a lifelong growth in mutual competency. And if they are already well into their marriage, they are simply deceiving themselves if they have become convinced that they are so competent with one another that there is nothing more to learn. Interpersonal sexual competency can be said to only begin when a couple has been together for a considerable amount of time. If we were just animals, that would not be the case. But we are human animals with fears, anxieties, needs, longings, and, above all, complex systems of meaning which interpret for us all the events of our life, particularly those that challenge us most directly as men and women. The real playmate is one who has achieved a high degree of competency in dealing with us because he (or she) shares our body, our spirit, our fantasy-life and our meaning systems. When we are put into a room with such a person and told that we have nothing else to do but make love, questions of competency are quite irrelevant.

Hence the essential prerequisite for growth in playfulness is the admission that we are not competent automatically and that we have to grow and learn what competency means with this other person. It is a hard admission to make, hard at the beginning of marriage and even harder as the years go on. For a man to admit to his wife, "I don't really know you. I don't really know how to make love to you," is a shattering experience. (Of course, it need not be expressed in those words.) For a woman to say to her husband, "You are a mystery to me. I have no real notion of how to please and satisfy you" is also shattering. Such admissions are an acceptance of the necessity for trust, confidence, respect, and affection to be established in some amount at least as an atmosphere conducive to the growth of sexual competence and playfulness. You can only admit that you are *not* good at something in the presence of another who is already sufficiently impressed by you that your admission of incompetence is not likely to diminish his respect for you. One can admit incompetence in most cases only in a set of circumstances where one can be reasonably confident that the other will increase rather than decrease his respect for you precisely because of the admission. If the man is convinced that when he says to his wife that he does not really understand how to make her happy, she will love him more, not less, his concession becomes relatively easy—though still painful. A woman will find it much easier to tell her husband that she needs to know much more about what is required to bring him pleasure (in bed and in the rest of their relationship) if she knows that his love will be deepened by such a request.

In other words, when we admit our lack of competence and our inadequacies in circumstances where there is already love and affection, then we are engaged precisely in that process of

self-disclosure and self-revelation which is already erotic play. The confession of inadequacy
and the desire to learn is already an act of sexual
playfulness—and in the proper circumstances an
intensely erotic one. "Show me how" is just about
the most seductive thing one can say to his sexual
partner, yet the words are so hard to say, they
stick so rigidly in our throat.

Playfulness also requires the freedom to learn
by mistakes, failures, and trial and error. If the
whole relationship depends on the success of
every experiment, then playfulness doesn't have
much of a life expectancy. A woman reads that a
sheer black bra will turn a man on, so she buys the
naughtiest one she can find and gives her husband
a good, long look at her in it one evening. He
seems mildly interested in how much it cost, but
is not aroused at all. If he were really sensitive, he
would of course catch what she was trying to do
and respond enthusiastically, if not to the gar-
ment, at least to her. No one is sensitive to every
cue all the time. If this failure so discourages the
woman that she is unwilling to risk other
"naughty" experiments, then there is simply not
enough trust and playfulness in the relationship
for the awkward trial and error growth, which is
the only way playfulness can expand and develop.

Similarly, a man finds himself intrigued by what
he has heard of some of the "French" techniques
of combining lovemaking and powerlessness. He
explains the techniques to his wife and she shows

a mild interest. They experiment and discover that the experience is considerably less for them than the wild, incredible pleasure the sex manuals promised. Both are bound to be somewhat disappointed, but if they can laugh the incident off and add it to the growing list of shared jokes the fund of trust and playfulness is great enough for their continued expansion and growth.

Techniques are relatively unimportant when compared with the fundamental dynamics of a relationship. Two human beings living in what is frequently oppressive intimacy make mistakes in dealing with each other every day. A thoughtless word, a joke that is intended to be funny but is cutting and hurtful, a burst of exasperation at the wrong time, a trivial complaint when tenderness is needed—these can be either laughed off or become part of the hidden agenda of frustration, anger and bitterness. Playfulness in bed and playfulness in the totality of a relationship mutually reinforce one another. Genital sexuality that is rigid and unimaginative inhibits the growth of playfulness in the common life, and a common life that is grim, serious, "responsible" and filled with mistakes, reprimands, and temper tantrums is not going to be transformed into play when the bedroom door closes.

Play is competitive. There is a certain kind of do-gooding mentality in the United States that thinks competition is Capitalist Immorality and that little children should learn to cooperate with one another instead of competing. Competition is part of the vitality of life. Little children compete and cooperate simultaneously in their games. They cannot compete unless they set up a framework of cooperation, and it is the enjoyment and challenge of competition that encourages them to sustain and improve the cooperation that provides the context of the game. What is wrong is the belief that you have to win all the time for the competition to be worth the effort. If the only fun in the game is winning, the game isn't much fun at all. No one can win all the time, and people who equate losing the game with failure in a wider sense miss the point of competition completely. (Incidentally, I find grammar school athletic programs repellent. Pick-up contests, sandlot games, ad hoc confrontations on the playing fields are great fun and part of growing up for both boys and girls. Well organized, uniformed, efficiently coached operations—like Little League, for example—are a serious business and designed more for parents than as healthy sport for children. These contests are so important to the parent because he, having lost all sense of playfulness, equates losing a game with failure in the real world.)

Part of the fun of the game is its competitiveness. "I top you, you top me;" "I'm better than you are, you're better than I am;" I can do something you can't do, you can do something I can't do." Indeed, the more fiercely competitive the game, the more fun it is for both sides because the more it challenges both to their maximum efforts. Only when the rules of the game are violated and the norms of the outside world are brought in does loss mean failure and defeat mean ignominy. Then, of course, one of the players will end the game and go home.

When a man and woman are cramped together in the narrow life space of their marriage there will be competition and conflict as they spar together for relative advantage over the limited resources that are available to them. Such conflict and competition is a way of working out tensions, of balancing needs, and of strengthening the bonds that hold the joint venture together. If the competition can be approached with the playfulness of the game world, where the competition is real indeed but not "serious" in the sense that the fundamental ego-strength and indispensable needs of either partner are being violated, then the bonds of cooperation are strengthened. They *struggle* together in order that they may struggle *together*. They contend with each other the way Jacob did with the angel of Yahweh, not in anger, not to tear the relationship apart, but in order to bind it together more solidly. The wrestling match between Jacob and the angel of Yahweh was indeed a wrestling match. God and Jacob were contending, fighting, competing with one another, but it was a competition that grew out of love and re-enforced that love.

Sexual competitiveness is indescribably erotic. If each partner is struggling to be better than the other sexually, it necessarily means that each is struggling to be better at giving pleasure to the other rather than taking it for oneself. It is the kind of competition in which everybody wins. If the husband has a particularly good night, in which his wife is at first reluctant and resistant and ends up almost pathetically pleading for more, he has won but so has she. If the wife drives out of her husband's mind all distractions, all thoughts of other women, indeed everything but desire for her by a scene that will haunt him for several days, she has triumphed indeed, but he has not exactly been a loser. To win a point in the sexual game is an absolute delight. "I showed him" or "I showed her" is a cry of exultation and self-satisfaction, but to lose a point by being shown is also a memorable experience.

Competition in the sexual game becomes un-healthy only under two circumstances: either one of the partners won't play, or one of the partners refuses to let the other play. In both cases all points are scored on one side, and the other is reduced, by his choice or by his partner's, to play-ing the role of passive cooperator. He becomes a respondent and audience who must react to and applaud the triumphs of the perennial victor. Some men's sexual egos are so weak that this is the only kind of game they are capable of playing. Their relationship with a woman must be an end-

less series of "scores." Some women are so
prudish, so passive, or so frightened that "to win"
a sexual tussle with a man would be to deny their
femininity. Such children, the conquering male
and the ever-conquered female, may blend together in a stable relationship, and presumably
worse things could happen to them. The man
might have married a woman who insists on
"scoring" sometimes herself, and she might have
married a man who wants to be challenged as well
as applauded and accepted. But such stable,
routine, one-way relationships ought not to be
confused with playfulness. Nobody wants to play
golf with the pro who shoots in the low 70s unless
he plays with an equalizing handicap. Sexual
competitiveness between a husband and wife enhances the sex gain only when there is relative
equality among the contestants, which means
that the husband must be brave enough to lose
some of the encounters and the wife brave
enough to win some of them.

The very use of the words "win" and "lose"
will be offensive to some. How can one speak of
winning and losing in something as intimate and
private as human love? It is not difficult if one
remembers that in the world of the game one's
success or failure as a human or as a man or
woman is in no way connected to whether one
wins or loses the game. The equations winning =
success, losing = failure are an invasion of the
world of the game by norms and values that do

not belong there. A husband and wife, involved in a deeply affectionate and playful sexual relationship with each other will have no problem at all understanding what I mean. The husband has many times experienced self-satisfaction, pride, and complacency as he drops off to sleep thinking "I really did it to her tonight," while the wife is falling asleep happily overwhelmed by an aggressive, demanding, absolutely implacable lover. Tonight she lost, but she had as much fun losing as he did winning.

For a woman to think to herself that this was her night for victory may well be even more exciting and rewarding than it would be for her husband. For in the culture in which she was raised, winning in sex is a male prerogative. To be able to win at the game is to show both the culture and her husband. She can be weak, passive, and surrendering when that is appropriate; she can be as fierce, demanding, impassioned, and as implacable as he when that is her mood.

Perhaps the most pleasurable kind of sexual play comes on those occasions when both the man and the woman are in aggressive, implacable moods. The competition then is indeed a fierce fight; it is Jacob wrestling with the angel of Yahweh. The struggle is wild, passionate, terrifying, indescribably enjoyable. Which of the partners "wins" may ultimately depend on the fine-tuned sensitivity of the other. If they are really skillful players at the sexual game they will be able to know when the other really ought to win, when at the last moment one substitutes graceful surrender for continued conflict. This is, of course, sexual playfulness refined to a high art. But the nice thing about having a lifetime playmate is that one has a long time to refine one's skills at the art. The equations of the sexual game may be unique in the game world—losing = winning, winning = winning. That's a game to bet on!

Playmates must be strong. They must refuse to take "no" for an answer (save on those occasions when their sensitivities reveal to them that "no" is reasonable with no diminution of love and trust). The playmate must have the vigor and the resourcefulness to tear away the masks and the defenses, the protections, the phony fears, the silly anxieties—all those escape hatches one uses to flee the terrors and delights of the sexual game. Strength requires confidence, of course, and a playmate who is not confident of his or her abilities to deal effectively with a sexual partner will not be much of a playmate. Conflict can coexist with the admission that one's competency needs to grow and develop. Indeed the assertion of omni-competence is normally an attempt to hide lack of confidence. The confident playmate says in effect, "There may still be much I have to learn about my spouse's fantasies, needs, desires, responses; but I know enough to be able to begin, and I am secure enough in our relationship to be able to move ahead." Confidence means that one is strong enough, secure enough, and knowledgeable enough to begin, knowing that afterwards the "playing by ear" that inevitably follows will not be a total failure. The problem for the man locked in the room with the Playmate of the Month that we discussed earlier is that he really doesn't know how to begin. How can he, since he is dealing with a stranger? Surely the first time a couple who have committed themselves to each other come together they too lack confidence, but they can both feel brave enough, strong enough, secure enough, accepted enough, loved enough to begin. Competency grows when confidence is a given.

But it is a given that needs constant re-enforcement. If we expect our sexual partner to become a playmate for us, we must constantly support, re-enforce, and build the partner's ego strength. A man needs to be told day in and day out that he is a good lover—even on those occasions when he is only adequate. A woman needs to hear, in season and out, that she is a totally gorgeous, desirable, seductive, irresistible female—even on those occasions when her awkwardness and hesitance make her quite resistible. A partner becomes a playmate to the extent that we successfully define him (or her) as such. A man cannot hear too often from his wife that she wants his body in hers; and she cannot hear too often from him that her breasts are so delectable that he simply cannot keep his hands off them.

To what extent must this pursuit of confidence and competence be explicit for the sexual game to flourish? Is it an art that can be pursued implicitly, tacitly, unreflectively? Or must it be something that is the subject of constant explicit dialogue and discussion within a relationship?

There are no clear and simple answers to these questions. Some people can develop an extraordinarily playful sexual relationship through skilled communication that is almost always subliminal and unobtrusive. Others can become easy and matter-of-fact in discussing the most intimate details of their lovemaking. Still others talk about it constantly, persuading themselves and boring others about their really great sex life when in fact they are blindly following the paradigms they find in the most recent manual. Finally, some people may be so tied in puritanical knots that they pretend most of the time that no such thing as sex exists in their life together. The style with which a couple pursues mastery of sexual playfulness depends upon the style of their personalities and the style of their relationship. Some talk too much, others not nearly enough. On balance it can be said that for most American couples the real risk is that they will not talk nearly enough.

To be "masterful" (or "mistressful") at the sexual game is to be in command of the situation, to be able to combine implacable firmness with sensitive tenderness, to know when to comfort, when to challenge, when to insist, when to defer, when to push, when to yield, when to become angry, when to reassure, when to win, when to lose, when to overwhelm, when to be over-whelmed, when to tear away resistance, and when to respect it. One can only learn these delicate arts by experimentation, practice, and attention to feedback. In the ordinary course of events most human beings gain mastery only to the extent that they focus self-conscious energy and effort on the process. It is not something that comes easily, naturally, or unreflectively.

To the argument that there are too many other obligations and responsibilities and important things in life to devote time to such a frivolous pursuit, one can only say that this is an option some people freely choose, but it is one that, in principle at least, is an obligation for no one. It may well be that there are other satisfactions in life that make sexual playfulness seem relatively unimportant. If that is the case for a given couple, so be it; but they are kidding themselves if they think that they have rejected an option that did not contain pleasure, variety, wonder, and re-ward. It is a good thing to be masterful, to feel that one has supreme and loving power over the other, that one can possess the other without his or her having the ability or the desire to resist. It is also good to know that one is under such tender but effective domination by another human being, that there is someone who can do with us whatever he or she wants, and that whatever he or she wants is what we want. Those who don't particularly care for such payoffs in their lives are within their rights in rejecting them, but they can scarcely dismiss as fools those who think otherwise.

A man puts his arm around his wife. She is limp, weary, depressed, and reluctant; it has been a hard day for her. His personality expands, blood rushes through his veins, his heart stirs because he knows that he has within himself the power to bring that limp body alive with pleasure and delight. It is not an absolutely necessary thing for a man to have such an experience, but it is a good thing, and for most men the more often they can have it, the better.

A woman sees her husband's face lined with care and preoccupation. There are a thousand and one troubled, anxious thoughts darting through his mind. She slips off her dress and exults in the power that is hers to so transform things that in a few moments there will be only one thing on his mind. When she is finished with him, the world will necessarily be brighter and warmer and more benign. It is not necessary for a woman to experience such exultation in her womanliness. Still it doesn't hurt, and most women cannot experience it too often. Playfulness, then, is not indispensable, but the question is why should anyone want to dispense with it?

To be playful in a sustained sexual relationship means to keep romance alive. Romance requires imagination, sympathy, understanding, persistence, sensitivity. It also requires physical tenderness. The frequency with which people make love depends on their tastes and needs. (Nine times a month is the American average, we are told.) But if physical tenderness is limited to just lovemaking, there is little romance left in the relationship. There are many times in the course of a life together when a gentle touch, a quick caress, a light kiss convey more passion, more romance, more commitment, and more playfulness than an extended romp in bed. The essence of playfulness is not so much that there is a necessity to do anything, but that there is an opportunity to do practically everything. Probably it is that absence of obligation and the presence of unlimited opportunity in sexual playfulness that most offends the puritans.

chapter 5

It ought to be easy to write about sexual fantasies. Everyone has them, and some are extremely vivid sexual daydreams. They have been the basis of all pornography and much great art, music, and literature (implicitly if not explicitly) in the course of human history. The current merchandisers of sexual fantasy show surprisingly little sophistication compared with many of their predecessors. As camera work, the photographs in *Playboy* may be excellent, but the fantasy they evoke is crude, gross, and unimaginative. It may appeal to the adolescent segment of the fantasy spectrum, but not to the more mature, nuanced, and subtle fantasy of lives of which even *Playboy* addicts are capable. Read, for example, Joseph

Conrad's description of lust in his *Outcast of the Islands* and compare it with a *Playboy* centerfold and decide which is more erotic.

But if sexual fantasy is universal, appealing and powerful, it is also a very awkward subject for discussion. Most people are ashamed of their fantasies, or they do not understand them. Many feel so guilty about them that they must vigorously deny them and launch angry attacks on those who hint of their existence. Some of the opposition to pornography, for example, is probably based on guilt about one's own vivid imagination. It seems that sexual fantasy is a subject which cannot be discussed coolly and dispassionately. Most of the systematic study and knowledge about fantasy life comes either from the psychiatrist's couch or from nonrandom and not necessarily representative interviews. We know only our own fantasies and are reluctant to believe that other people may have the same images in their imaginations. Psychologists understand very dimly the purpose and functioning of human fantasy life—sexual or otherwise, although they agree that it is the source of art, poetry, and religious symbols and it is of critical importance in the development of both human personality and human social culture.

Our fantasy lives are wild, disordered, chaotic. To speak of them in any systematic fashion is to impose an order and organization on them which is totally absent in reality. The fantasy world is infantile. It is, to use Norman O. Brown's phrase, "polymorphously perverse." It draws the line at no sexual behavior, because it has not learned like the ego that certain kinds of sex are destructive of human relationships, human society, human civilization. Incest, rape, homosexuality, bestiality, sadomasochistic orgies are all completely undifferentiated in the raw and primal imagination.

Contrary to Professor Brown I do not believe that the polymorphously perverse infantile sexual imagination can be taken as a norm for adult life. The human race turned polymorphously perverse would quickly extinguish itself. Nonetheless we must cope with our sexual fantasies. They are part of the ambiguity of the human condition. The strain between polymorphous perversity and mature self-restraint is one of the most fundamental of ambiguities. Neither of these polarities can be eliminated without destroying the personality.

Are sexual fantasies evil? As fantasies, surely not; they are the natural activity of the imagination of incarnate sexual beings. They become evil when we attempt to actually accomplish all of them (which happens usually only among the unbalanced), or when we permit them to substitute for relationships in the world occupied by real human beings. Some fantasies can be carried out into the real world; other fantasies give us critical hints about our personality and our needs; and still others can provide a richness and variety in our sexual relations that may substantially improve our emotional life and our psychological well-being. Finally, sexual fantasy has profoundly religious overtones. It is part of the preconscious self that produces both sexual and religious images, which are inextricably linked in many cases in the same symbol.

Such a suggestion is offensive to puritans. How can something as filthy as "dirty thoughts" be religious? The God that made us with a wild, uncontrollable fantasy life obviously made an artistic mistake. He made an even greater mistake when he permitted the preconscious, from which the grossest sexual images emerge, to also produce the most elevated religious symbols.

To add to the complexities of attempting to discuss sexual fantasies and their role in the relationship between husband and wife, it is impossible to discuss fantasies without describing them. Such descriptions are necessarily erotic, and the pages on which they are written have a tendency to get steamy. Both the puritan and the prurient (and puritans are usually cryptoprurients) can't get beyond the steam. I hasten to add that the fantasies presented in this chapter are tame. Any reader who claims that he or she does not have such fantasies (indeed some that are much wilder) is simply not telling the truth (or perhaps not admitting it to himself or herself).

Despite the complexities of discussing sexual fantasies, the discussion must take place. They are part of the human condition, and to pretend they are not is to ignore the facts. They are part of human sexuality, and an attempt to provide meaning for human sexuality that passes over them is bound to be inadequate. They tell us something critical about the nature and destiny of humankind, and a theology which ignores such data is a theology with blinkers on.

I will confine my discussion to heterosexual fantasies because for most people they are by far the most frequent and because they are the most pertinent to the subject of marriage and sexual play. To wrestle with other kinds of fantasies would take us far afield and muddy even more a complex and intricate subject. Still it must be noted in passing that a mature person knows that sexuality is a continuum and not a sharp dichotomy. A sexually mature man is confident enough in his own maleness that he does not have to try to hide from himself that he sometimes finds the bodies of other men in a shower room sexually appealing. Nor need a women feel that she is perverted because she occasionally feels a strong urge to play with the breasts of another woman. Such feelings, longings, urges are normal statistically and psychologically. To acknowledge them is merely to concede the complexity of human sexuality. Mature heterosexuals do not take such urges as a norm for action; they do not feel constrained to give in to such longings, and they are not shaken by insecurity or guilt simply because they discover such desires in themselves.

As far as one can judge from the sparse, confused, and uneven psychiatric and social scientific literature on the subject, there are four general kinds of frequent sexual fantasies. Each is as prevalent in men as in women, although they may take different forms in the different sexes.

1) *Fantasies of nakedness.* Dressing and undressing is a primordial human behavior that is filled with sexual implications and overtones beginning with the very earliest childhood memories. To be exposed is to be seen, enjoyed, possessed. Clothes are designed both to conceal and to reveal, to hide and to display. The sexual implications of clothes are so obvious that one should not have to mention it. But the very hint that dressing and undressing are highly sexual activities is enough to send puritans into paroxysms of anger.

Indeed the sexual power of taking off and putting on clothes is so great that lovers in a sustained relationship must develop an (usually) implicit agreement as to when such activity may be permitted to be overtly sexual and when the sexual content of it will be ignored. Otherwise they would be late for every appointment that they had to keep together. Such a modus vivendi may deprive dressing and undressing of any explicit connotation, and undressing may become as casual and insignificant as turning on the TV set. A good criterion of the playfulness of a sexual relationship is the richness, the excitement, the significance that a husband and wife permit the ordinary but highly charged activity of putting on and taking off clothes to be. It is a behavior that is inherently playful with an almost limitless variety of playful possibilities. When all play is gone out of it, there can be little play left in the relationship. If the nightly ritual has become routine in the real world, undressing or being undressed is still pure terror and pure delight in the world of dream and fantasy.

2) *Rape and being raped.* I hesitate to use the word, because real rape is a sordid, violent, ugly, vicious act. It may occasionally be that in fantasy life too, but fantasy "rape" is transformed and has little in common with the ugly violation of another human being that occurs all too frequently in the real world. For it is of the essence of fantasy rape that one is forced to do something that one desperately wants to do, or that one forces the other to do something that the other deeply wants to do. There may be violence in fantasy rape but not violation. One may be powerless (or render another powerless) but it is a pleasurable and not a brutalized powerlessness. To the extent that brutality may be involved, it is a brutality that brings delight and not shame. The essence of fantasy rape is that resistance, inhibition, hesitancy are firmly and completely swept away. One either becomes powerless and is completely at the whim of the other or renders the other powerless and has complete control of him (or her).

3) *Seduction and being seduced.* Rape fantasies

concentrate on the direct, forcible, and, if need be, violent reduction of resistance. Seduction fantasies focus on the slow, gentle art of taking possession of or being possessed by the other. Instead of the process's being quick, firm, even harsh, it is long, teasing, and leisurely. The end is the same, of course, but the important fact of the imagery is not the end but the style, the modality. In both the rape and seduction fantasies one conquers or is conquered. In the former one's competency is directed at immediate conquest, in the latter it is directed at slow, gradual, agonizingly delightful surrender.

4) *Fantasies that have to do with variety of position, place, and organs involved.* Given that there is an almost limitless variety of places where sex can occur and a considerable number of positions and techniques for obtaining sexual satisfaction with one's partner, there are countless possibilities for fantasies on this subject. Most marital sex takes place in one position, in one place, and with one technique, but this does not prevent the imagination from contemplating a wide variety of interesting possibilities.

Such a list of fantasies is bound to be inadequate and incomplete, but to sketch some of the fantasies that are apparently so frequent as to be universal may tell us something extremely important about human sexuality.

Let us now consider the fantasies of a relatively typical (composite) upper middle-class American couple. I wish to emphasize that these fantasies are "normal" both in the statistical sense of being commonplace and in the psychological sense of not indicating emotional disturbance. On the contrary, such fantasies (or fantasies like them) are typical to the point of being almost universal among physically healthy adults.

The wife imagines herself being brought to a party of her husband's friends. The men are all wearing evening clothes, and she is wearing a black strapless gown and black lace underthings. Her husband begins to describe quite clinically her sexual attributes. His friends demand evidence and he compels her to slowly remove her clothes. He makes appropriate descriptive comments as she undresses, and his friends applaud in appreciation. Completely naked, she is then compelled to walk among the men while they touch and caress her, leaving not a part of her body untouched. Finally, her husband makes love to her while his friends cheer them on. Her fantasy ends as he turns her over to one of his friends for his pleasure.

The husband is on an airplane on a business trip. He is seated next to an attractive, extremely shapely woman with pale white skin, dark hair turning slightly gray, and a deep seductive voice. In his fantasy she strikes up a conversation, letting her hand wander to his thigh and leaning her body suggestively against his. As they get off the airplane, she invites him to her hotel room. In the room he becomes completely passive and she assumes control of the situation, teasing him to uncontrollable desire. She then kneels astride him and screams with joy as she brings the two of them to a dazzling climax. (In the real world, of course, she gets off the plane without saying a word.)

The wife is in the kitchen finishing up the dishes in early afternoon. She imagines a man entering the room. He is dark, muscular, hard, and clad only in a scanty loin cloth. Without saying a word he comes up behind her and locks his arms around her in a fierce embrace. She tries to break away, but her struggles are useless. He kisses the back of her neck and her shoulders, squeezes her breasts and tightens his grip on her. She stops struggling. Still silent, he unzips her dress, tears away her panties and bra and forces himself into her—quickly, skillfully, and insistently. She has never before responded so completely and totally to a man. She is utterly helpless and totally transformed. She can almost feel his hot breath on her face when the phone rings and brings her out of her daydream.

Her husband is having lunch by himself. The waitress is young, pretty, with an air of intelligence and good breeding. He imagines waiting for her after work and inviting her for a drink. They have a fascinating and very intellectual conversation—as well as several drinks. They drive to a deserted place and he begins to kiss and caress her. She resists, pleads with him to stop, but he gets his mouth on her nipple and then his penis between her thighs. She surrenders, giving herself to him completely and totally. Her body responds to his as a custom-made glove fits her hand. On the way back to the city she clings to him and makes him promise that he will do it to her again. In the real world he pays his check, leaves an extra large tip and departs.

His wife is on the beach, watching the children play near the water. The bronzed young lifeguard is the only other adult in sight. In fantasy the children leave and she approaches the young man. He nervously keeps his eyes away from her as they talk. Her hand rests on his knee and then slides up to his trunks. He looks up at her, a mixture of fear and longing in his eyes. Her lips meet his just as she unhooks the top of her swimming suit. Their two bodies merge on the sand as the waters of the lake wash over them. One of the children intrudes into the daydream with a demand for a drink of water.

Her husband is having a Scotch in the golf course locker room, waiting for his foursome partners to finish their showers. In fantasy he sees through the wall into the women's shower room. He is then dragged into the locker room and pinned against the wall by a group of women in various advanced stages of undress. At the direction of a tall, athletic woman with large breasts and leopard skin shorts, they take off his clothes and tie him to a bench. The women all gather round, playing with him, kissing him, pinching him, tickling him, making fun of him. They push their breasts against his lips and make him suck on them; they take turns lying on top of him. Finally they drag him into the shower and have a merry time covering him with soapsuds and hugging and embracing his now wet and slippery body. Before the fantasy goes any further (and he is perfectly prepared to go on and on with it) the friends arrive and the post-golf poker game begins.

Note well that we are dealing with two responsible, self-possessed adults. They are good parents, good spouses. The husband would no more rape the young waitress than he would jump off the top of a building. The wife would no more put her hand on the lifeguard's sexual organs than she would put it in a fire. They are not sick or dirty people. Their fantasies—vivid, exciting, and compelling —come out of their experiences and imaginations and are stored up in their unconscious and preconscious minds. If they were hypnotized (which is in itself another fantasy) and compelled to live out their fantasies, they would find it a delightful experience (who wouldn't?) only because they could then be dispensed from freedom of choice, responsibility, and guilt. They are much like the young man in Eric Rohmer's *Chloe in the Afternoon*. In his fantasy life he had a secret power which forced every woman he wanted to bed down with him instantly. But when the very real Chloe became available to him, he fled in panic to return to his wife—who, Rohmer skillfully hints, had fled herself from a similar fantasy turned disturbingly real.

What then are fantasies besides entertaining ways of passing the time? They are first of all a way to release emotional and psychic energy, dangerous only if they become so compulsively important that real human relationships and responsibilities are ignored, or if one seriously begins to turn the fantasies into reality. Daydreams probably have a function not unlike real dreams: they are a harmless way of discharging certain kinds of pent-up energy. In order for the personality to develop a firm core, for society to protect its culture and structure, for human civilization to survive, humankind must learn to divert, channel, restrain, and focus its raw, primal energies. These energies do not go away. In principle we would still like to be able to make love to everyone we find desirable (which, it turns out, includes a very substantial number of potential partners). In practice this is not possible, and we would be afraid of it if it were, but our polymorphously perverse infantile libido is still there and finds outlets for its longings in images, dreams, and fantasies.

But these fantasies also reveal to us—if we are not ashamed to consider their implications—that we are creatures with powerful, deep, complex hungers. We can restrain and control these hungers, but we cannot eliminate them completely and it is a mistake to try. Intimate relationships exist, from one point of view, as safety-valve mechanisms in which some of the raw force of our primal hunger can be discharged in a context of safety and support. Sexual intimacy creates a context in which some of the energy of our sexual fantasy lives can be expended in safe and constructive ways. The more relaxed and playful the intimacy the easier it is to let the fantasy imp out of the bottle sometimes. In such circumstances the imp not only does not destroy the relationship but enhances it. Intimacy releases fantasy; fantasy reenforces intimacy.

The matron on the beach yearns in fantasy to hold and caress and kiss the penis of the young lifeguard. Indeed, if she is able to be frank with herself, there are many, many penises that she would like to kiss. That obviously is not to be, but her husband's sexual organs are available to be kissed whenever she wishes. He is not likely to mind, or if he prudishly resists at first she can overcome his reluctance. There is no reason why she cannot hold and kiss him every day even if they do not make love. It is not necessary that she do so, of course, but the option is available to her. Out of fear or uncertainty or shame, she may not try; she may even resist when he urges her. No one would argue that the marriage is endangered or that the sexual relationship is no good. The point is that there are a host of ways in which a woman can act out some of her fantasies in a playful relationship with her husband if she wants to do so. To systematically reject all these possibilities is to lock up raw energies which might be constructively and healthily released. There are other ways to release such energies (and celibates can constructively focus them in other directions). Still, for sexual partners it seems foolish not to exploit the potentiality for focusing fantasy energy in exciting, challenging, and delightful playfulness.

Her husband was delighting in his women's shower room fantasy until the poker game began. In the unlikely eventuality that a couple of women actually would drag him into a shower, he would be acutely embarrassed (though he probably wouldn't run away). Chances are that his fantasy will not come true, but a warm, soapy, stimulating shower with his wife is another matter altogether. She might resist at first, but if he is afraid to ask, afraid to try, afraid to insist (as many men are), then an opportunity for playfulness that would creatively release some of his fantasy energy has been passed by. The marriage won't end; he may not even be sexually frustrated; but a marriage composed entirely of such missed opportunities will become dull precisely because there is so little emotional energy invested in it.

Fantasy, then, does not provide a detailed outline for reality, but it does open up some interesting possibilities. What possibilities will be pursued depends on the people involved. In the nature of things some relationships can only sustain a relatively limited amount of fantasy discharge and sharing. For either partner to push beyond what the traffic will bear is unwise. On the other hand, some couples can develop a very full, elaborate and detailed mutual fantasy life. On balance, there is probably room in most relationships for more shared fantasy than actually exists.

To what extent can one share fantasies with another? Some fantasies are intensely private and simply can't be shared. Others can be shared or not depending on the state of the relationship. Others can be shared with relative ease. There are no hard and fast rules; so much depends on the taste, the sense of humor, the self-possession, the emotional strength of the people involved. Certainly the direct encounter group strategy of "Let's sit down now and communicate with each other about our fantasy lives. You tell me yours, and I'll tell you mine" is both foolish and harmful. Fantasies are more likely to be shared in slow gradual self-revelation as a total relation grows in trust and expands in affection. To make them a primary, explicit, and direct item on the mutual agenda is not likely to serve much purpose. Sharing fantasies is no magical cure for a relationship that has serious problems. It is more likely to be an addition to a relationship that is healthy and developing.

Some couples may elaborate several separate fantasy worlds which they can explore together— Turkism harem, Greek slave market, Roman bath, etc. Others may find such highly developed shared fantasies bizarre and kinky. For still others the fantasy sharing may be rather limited and implicit but still important. One husband discovered mostly by guesswork that his wife had a thing about men unbuttoning her blouse. When she wore a blouse it was usually a sign that she was sexually hungry, a sign of which she was unaware. His rather acute sensitivities had picked it up and, although he never talked to her about it, he became quite practiced at unbuttoning blouses, doing so in many unusual places despite some initial resistance on her part. It was a small skill and a small sharing of imagination carried on at a low level of explicit communication. It did not transform the relationship; it did not save the marriage from any threat; but it did make their life together somewhat more playful, and it did improve somewhat the quality of their life together. In all human relationships, however, the "somewhat" may turn out to be cumulatively more important than the big breakthroughs.

I must emphasize that fantasy-sharing is an option, not an obligation. There is no all-purpose formula for what ought to be shared or how. Given the fact that most people are so ashamed and so guilty about their fantasy lives, it is likely that fantasy-sharing in most relationships will be minimal. I would be suspicious, indeed, of those who contend that they have a great big and very easy fantasy-sharing thing going. My inclination would be to suspect that there is something profoundly wrong with the marriage and the huge fantasy success is a cover up. Slow, gradual, tasteful, witty sharing of daydreams is probably a sign of a healthy development. Anything else ought to be considered dubious.

Still the daydreams are there, and while we do not act on all of them, they are a relatively important part of our lives. They reveal the variety, the depth, the confusion, the complexity, the passion, the longing of our personalities. They provide some outlet for our psychic energies, they enrich our lives, and, although they may also occasionally drive us to distraction, they frequently provide the raw material for deepening and strengthening long-term sexual commitments. Some of us can use them as the source for artistic creation, and all of us use them for consolation, support, and strengthening the ego.

There are two critical conclusions to be drawn from our reflections about sexual fantasies. First of all, no one is dull. The imagination is active, ingenious, creative, energetic. If we are dull in our sexual relations and in the totality of our lives it is because we repress the variety and ingenuity of our imaginations. Dullness is something that is chosen and accepted, not something built into our natures and personalities. Only when the fantasy world has been completely suppressed does dullness become a chronic affliction.

Finally, the polymorphous perversity of our imagination reveals us as creatures hungering for

the absolute in fulfillment and love. Not to be able
to make love to everyone we would like to is a
frustration for a being who yearns for the Ultimate
in possession and being possessed. The infantile
primordial energies stirring up constantly in our
ids represent the longing of the human spirit to
break out of the constraints and limitations that
separate it from the rest of the cosmos and to find
loving, consuming union with all that is and All
That Is. The man who imagines himself being
played with in the women's locker room is at a
deep psychological level yearning to be played
with once again by his mother. But at an even
deeper existential level he is yearning for union
through surrender to the ultimate maternal power
of the universe. The woman lusting for the body of
the young lifeguard may be psychologically seeking for the sexual organs of her father, but exis-
tentially she is seeking to possess and be possessed
by the ultimate paternal power of the universe.
Our fantasy life reveals the deep wound in the human personality that was created by our being
surrendered in existence as beings who are not
Being. But it is through that wound that Being re-
turns with the offer of love and unity.

Thus when a man and woman who are committed to developing a sustained sexual intimacy
with each other begin to share their fantasies, they
are at the same time sharing their own longings
for ultimate union, which in the Christian perspective is Ultimate Union.

What the world of the resurrection will be like we do not know. We used to write off as heathen foolishness the Islamic vision of a paradise of sensual delights. But that vision may not be without insight. That loving unity towards which our sexual fantasies awkwardly grope will be enjoyed in the world of the resurrection. Will it be different from our imaginings? Surely. But it will be different because it will be better.

Eye has not seen nor ear heard, nor has it entered into the heart of man. . .

chapter 6

Sexual play is not only fantastic it is also festive. In the early stages of humankind there was but one thing to be celebrated: life itself. Our hold on life then was precarious, but because of our marvelous technological powers we modernists are not aware of how tenuous our hold on life still is and how remarkable is the miracle of daily survival. Our ancestors could not afford the illusion that the survival of life was commonplace.

And so they celebrated each new evidence that in the struggle between order and chaos, between life and death, life and order had won another round. The festivals were festivals of life, of the birth of young animals, of the first fruits, of harvest, of vintage, of planting, of the returning sun in

its annual circuit from north to south. (The Jewish
Passover Feast, become the Christian Easter, was
a spring fertility festival. The paschal lamb represented the first fruit of the flocks, and the unleav-
ened bread the first fruit of the fields. Christmas,
the feast of light, replaced the pagan feast of the
return of the sun. The Ember Days, those pagan
residuals of an era when man was closer to nature,
represented feasts of planting, first fruits, harvest,
and vintage. Memorial Day, Labor Day, Thanksgiving may be rough secular equivalents.) When
the young animals were born, the first fruits har-
vested, the grapes picked, our primitive ancestors
felt that they were participating in and continuing
the primal conflict between life and death, between order and chaos, which occurred at the beginning of the cosmos and from which the ordered
world had taken its beginning. The spring festival
and the harvest festival were profoundly religious
celebrations of life. In such celebrations our ancestors united themselves with the gods and their
battle against chaos, sought the gods' blessing on
their work, and perhaps also passed on to their
children the secret lore of the field and the flocks.
For since planting and tilling and bringing to
harvest were religious activities, so the knowledge
of how this ought to be done was religious too.

In these celebrations, sex and religion were
mixed so as to be indistinguishable. The festivals
were festivals of life and fertility, and of course
the most powerful life force in themselves and in

other creatures that humans knew was sex. It
was fertility that continued the flocks, reproduced
the fields each year and kept their own clan or
tribe or village going even when individuals died.
Sex was evidently, indisputably sacred. Sacred
celebrations then were necessarily sexual.

The orgy of the Roman Saturnalia (which we
keep alive if not at Christmas then surely at New
Year) was merely a late and secularized version
of the primitive notion that on feasts when life
was celebrated one should let all the forces of
life run wild and free. Sexual abandon at the time
of celebration was a way of celebrating and a way
of uniting oneself with the powerful life forces.
Sexual intercourse in the newly planted fields was
a magical attempt to link the fundamental life
forces of the universe with the life of the tribe
and the village and its crops. There is some evidence that in remote parts of European mountain
regions (Spain, France, Yugoslavia, Italy, Hun-
gary) the custom of intercourse in the fields survived even into the first part of this century.
Archaic people, who viewed all of life as organic,
did not draw sharp distinctions between the fertility of their own bodies and that of their fields;
they were both part of the fundamental life-giving
force of the cosmos.

That sex was celebration and that celebration
was sexual was so self-evident to archaic people
that they would not even have thought to question
it. (I know of one young man who was blessed

with the splendid nickname, "Spuds." His parents in an outburst of playfulness uncharacteristic of their people had deliberately and consciously decided that he ought to be conceived in a potato field in Ireland. How his nickname will be explained to Spuds when he begins to ask where he got it is a problem for his parents to contend with.) Civilization, technology, puritanism, Enlightenment rationality have all but broken this organic thread of life celebration. Even if we repair that thread and begin to see that our food, our bodies, our cosmos all emerge from one supremely powerful life-giving process we would do so self-consciously, reflectively, deliberately. There are advantages to that, of course. Unlike our primitive ancestors we can reflect on and understand more deeply these primal unions. We can express them not only in music, art, poetry, and dance but also in philosophy, theology, and social science. We have paid for our sophistication by falling from a certain level of innocence, and by its very nature reflection makes us self-conscious and deprives us of unsophisticated spontaneity.

Sex, for our archaic ancestors, was necessarily public. There was no way the life-giving forces could be hidden, covered, prettied-up. Sexual intercourse even among primitive peoples usually took place in some sort of privacy (though it meant something different to them than to us, no doubt). But conception and reproduction were public events frought with powerful and deeply religious implications. Public or quasi-public intercourse on great religious feasts served to remind the members of the tribe that sexual relationships were not just personal, private affairs to be carried out between men and women in carefully secluded secrecy. It prolonged the existence of the tribe and united it with the basic creative processes of the cosmos. Sex was both a celebration and an event to be celebrated.

Mind you, all of this was ritualistic and objective. Sexual play and celebration were enacted in song and dance, the basic parameters of which were very carefully regulated by the historic traditions. The internal selves of the people involved in the ritual were not necessarily affected. One engaged in festive behavior and was perhaps carried away by it to experience it deeply and internally, but it was a very unself-conscious form of personal involvement. No more was required or possible, because the person was not sharply distinct from the rest of the organism that was the village or the tribe. The question of whether the sexual play that was part of the religious celebration was self-fulfilling or not would have been totally meaningless to primitive celebrants. It would never have occurred to them to ask whether "I'm getting anything out of this celebration."

A man and woman engaging in intercourse in a field they had just planted may have enjoyed the experience above and beyond what was required by the ritual. But the game was played according to its rubrics whether they personally felt playful or not. Indeed, their own internalized playfulness was scarcely to the point. In the objective order their sexual play was far more developed than our own, but subjective playfulness could easily be minimal and indeed it was neither required nor understood. If one unself-consciously intuits the connections between all life-giving forces, then the abandonment of oneself to the interplay of those forces is equally unself-conscious. Subjective play may not have been possible in those archaic societies, but then it was not necessary. In our own age, playfulness is either subjectively enjoyed or we do not define it as play at all. On the whole I think this is progress, but it is progress that makes life far more complicated. (Compare the farmer and his wife copulating in the field in order to keep the ancient ritual magic alive with Spud's parents in the rain-soaked potato field—I presume it was rain-soaked; Ireland is always rain-soaked. The former couple continue the ancient practice they do not understand and on which they do not reflect, because of a desperate hope that their actions will improve the chances of a good crop, on which their lives, or at least their prosperity, depend. The latter are engaging in an act of pure merriment, not to say devilment. It seems to be simply a hell of a lot of fun to conceive your first child in a potato field in the land of his predecessors. Both couples are keeping a tradition alive, one objectively and unself-consciously, the other subjectively and unself-consciously in a burst of euphoria. We self-conscious moderns have a difficult time getting into the heads of the farmer and his wife, but we have little trouble understanding Spud's parents. We may think they're crazy; we may envy them; but we certainly know what they are up to.)

One of the differences between us and our archaic ancestors is that for all our talk about sexual permissiveness and openness we have privatized and profaned sex. Intercourse is now something that takes place between two human beings without any implications for anyone else in the society. What they do is their business (unless they are contributing to the population explosion). It is an event that may have deep meaning for them, but it has no particular meaning for the rest of us. Indeed, there is no direct way they can share it with us, especially when a child does not result from their union—and nowadays children result only in carefully regulated numbers. Society truly does not intrude on their sex life the way it used to. There is also no way their sex life can be related to the rest of humankind. Privatism is a two-edged sword: it protects you from outside intrusion but prohibits you (at least inhibits you) from sharing. Unprivatized sex may be part of celebrations, even religious celebrations. It may become part of public play, albeit highly objectified and ritualized play. Privatized sex does not participate in public celebrations and is sharply separated from religious ritual. It is very difficult for privatized sex to maintain its festive and celebratory characteristics. Hence, of course, it becomes profane. We may sacralize the sexual union with a marriage ceremony and perhaps frequent renewals of the marriage vows, but the sacred is invoked in these ways to create a distant and legalistic context. It does not represent the life-giving powers of the cosmos and does not permeate in awe and mystery the ongoing union between man and woman. Sex is no longer part of public celebration. Nor is it set in a context of sacred and religious festivity. The man and woman have been freed from the ties of both church and state, tribe and cult. What they do now is their own business; only, unfortunately, desacralized, privatized sex can easily become dull, uneventful and monotonous. The web of meaning that supported sex in its objective playfulness has been sundered. The burden, then, is almost entirely on the man and woman themselves to create a web of meaning of their own, in which subjective playfulness can grow and in which sexual celebration can survive when it is enjoyed subjectively.

The problem is yet to be considered seriously. Some free love communards and other counterculture types have tried to recreate the fluidity and the dynamism of archaic sexual celebration, as though one could instantaneously and by freely chosen social contract reconstruct the archaic world, which has been irrevocably lost. Many men and women have their own "mini celebrations" in which birthdays, anniversaries, special commemorations become occasions for special and more elaborate sexual interchanges. A few couples set aside a day, a night, or a weekend a couple of times a year for their own very private and very much do-it-yourself "ember day." There are also certain days during the year—particularly, I suspect, Christmas and New Year's Eve when the atmosphere of sexual encounter between husband and wife is deliberately and self-consciously transformed. In this way one may involve oneself in a celebration that is widespread and public, but it must be noted that all of these sexual celebrations are optional and up to the individual couple to decide whether they will occur or not or whether they are celebratory or not. Finally, the notion that lovemaking unites the couple not only with each other but with the rest of humankind and with the fertility of the cosmos—a notion that was so obvious and unquestionable to our ancestors —rarely even occurs to contemporary men and women.

Play is festive by its very nature. It is enjoyable; it is a celebration of human strength, dignity, and integrity, and affirmation that human creative forces can triumph over disorder, confusion, and death. Sociologist Peter Berger quite properly points out that play is a "rumor of angels," "a hint of the transcendent," a signal of what the universe means, a blunt, brilliant, brave affirmation on the part of humankind that death will not snuff out our dazzling creativity. The player, like the unconscious, is confident of his own immortality. In the world of play he shuts out as unreal the thought of death, of nothingness, of oblivion.

The game is serious, but it is not deadly serious. On the contrary it is vitally serious, because the game is a celebration of life over death. Play that is not celebratory is just not play; and sex without a celebratory dimension will become grim, somber, and deadly serious. For a man and woman sex will become a celebration or it can never be playful.

But what is there to celebrate? This is unfortunately a question that all too many married people ask with deadly seriousness. We celebrate the fact that we are alive; that we can eat and drink, sleep and wake, and make love; that we have family and friends; that the sun rises, the moon shines, the rain falls, the sky is blue; that there is food to eat and wine (beer, vodka, gin, Scotch, Irish mist, bourbon, etc., etc.) to drink. We celebrate the good times together and our surviving the bad times, the mistakes we have learned from, the growth we have experienced, the joy and the delight and the pleasure we are able to take in one another's bodies.

The demanding, responsible routine of upper middle-class professional lives leaves us little time to enjoy, little time to realize that there are things to be enjoyed, and practically no time to celebrate that which we have enjoyed. Can one imagine anything less celebratory than a suburban Christmas cocktail party? The light of the world has come indeed!

Sex, then, is a celebration of both its own over-whelming pleasure and power and all the other good things that the powers of light and life have made available to us. When someone says that he or she is too tired or too worn out at the end of the day to have anything to celebrate, it may well be that the absolute truth is spoken. But this is not a judgment on the things in the universe which ought to be celebrated or on the celebratory power of sexual intercourse. It is merely a reflection on how oppressingly, stultifyingly dull the person has permitted his (or her) life to become. If we cannot see that there is anything to celebrate, if the cares, worries, distractions, and responsibilities of our common life have blinded us to the appropriateness and the possibility and necessity of celebration, heaven knows sex will not be playful. What's to celebrate? What's to be festive about? Why play?

And so, absentmindedly, casually, unreflectively, husband and wife make love. It is a private, profane encounter carried out with little sense of awe, reverence, or mystery. It unites them temporarily to each other, but it has no implications for their relationship with the rest of humankind, the cosmos, or the Primal Power. Technically competent they may be, physiologically and perhaps psychologically satisfied they may also be, but good God in heaven, playful they are not.

Sex is expansive. It increases, quite marginally, it is true, the amount of space our body occupies; it speeds up our physiological processes—heartbeat, blood flow, hormone secretion; it increases our physical energy and the madcap productivity of our imagination. It seems to fill us up until we are quite literally ready to burst. It also normally induces an emotional as well as physical "high." Our personalities expand at the same time. We feel bigger, more dynamic, more uninhibited. We are psychologically as well as physically excited, challenged, expanded.

When a man takes the body of his woman, when every inch of her flesh momentarily belongs to him, his sense of dignity, pride, masculinity and power is elevated and transformed, or at least there is a strong strain in the encounter towards such a transformation. And when a woman is locked in an embrace with her man, when the last tatters of inhibition and restraint are put aside, her sense of elegance, beauty, fullness, strength, and power are dramatically enhanced, or at least the strain toward such enhancement is there. At such a time, pride in being a man or a woman and gratitude that one is a man or a woman become very strong. One can resist such pride and gratitude; one can deny it, one can repress it with guilt, prudery, disgust, or even hatred, but still the

physiological and psychological forces are at work
and draw both lovers toward pride and gratitude
in each other as well as toward a raw and fundamental sense of pride in themselves.

Sex is an act of gratitude whether it is enjoyed
or recognized. It is a celebration of the goodness
in being a man or a woman, the goodness that is
in being human with a capacity for sexual union.
Sex is not merely communion; it is also Eucharist.
It is an act of thanksgiving to the other, to the
self, to whatever power there may be in the universe that has made this goodness possible.

One can certainly drain most of this communion
and Eucharist dimension out of sex. Celebration
can be denied, ignored, refused; but it is still there.
It would be a mistake to underestimate the human
capacity to de-romanticize everything, to reduce
even the most exciting events to the mundane and
the commonplace. It would be even more a mistake to underestimate the capacity of the human
creature to contend that such routinization is realism, wisdom, virtue, sophistication. In a desacralized, privatized world a contemporary human can
get away with both routinization and its justifi-
cation. Sex is ordinary; it is commonplace; it is
unromantic, unsentimental, unexciting. There is
in it nothing of communion, nothing of Eucharist,
of ceremony, of celebration. Besides, there is a
hard day to face tomorrow at the office, the club,
the school. The feel of lips, neck, belly, thigh,
buttocks has no meaning other than pleasurable

sensation. One can touch a breast, stroke an arm, nibble on an ear, squeeze a rear end, run one's fingers through hair and still experience nothing more than localized sensation as a prelude to effective tension release. Celebration, communion, Eucharist? Don't be silly.

Okay, if that's the way you want it. But let it be clear that this sober realism, or puritanical or other quasi-religious variations of it, are entirely interpretations that the people involved choose to put on the event—a meaning they elect to assign to it for reasons of fear, infidelity, or shame that are all their own. There are other interpretations possible, perhaps harder to sustain but also infinitely more rewarding. Such interpretations do not deny that local sensation or tension release are involved, but they suggest that the immediate sensation is a revelation of something else, of love, of gratitude, fidelity, commitment, which may be focused indeed through the common life into the orgasmic embrace, but also out through the common life to place humankind, the cosmos and whatever Power may have produced the cosmos. Playfulness simply cannot be sustained in a sexual relationship unless some one of these other interpretive schemes is applied to the lovemaking event. A woman's breast may simply be a sensitive gland that a man enjoys touching and a woman enjoys having touched. Or it may be a revelation of grace, love, and elegance in her, certainly, but also in the world of which she and her husband are a part. One can take one's interpretive position anywhere along the continuum between these two extremes, but the closer one gets to the second, the more likely sex is to be celebratory and hence playful. To unzip a zipper may be only that, or it may be the doorway to a place of excitement, delight, and pleasure. Which it is finally depends on how we choose to define it. And that definition and our acting on it will determine whether we are playmates or just mates.

The religious copout defines sex not as celebration, communion, and Eucharist, but for having children, rearing children, reducing concupiscence, keeping passions under control, and avoiding infidelity within the strictures of marriage. It is something best not talked about; it is animal, worldly, bodily; an embarrassment, disgrace, a regrettable necessity, or perhaps a necessary evil. (As St. Augustine suggests, it is at best a venial sin.) It is base, low, carried out in the same regions of the body where excretion takes place (*inper faces et urinam nascimur,* as the pagan poet so elegantly puts it). To use such words as "communion" or "Eucharist" concerning it is either romantic or idealistic or sacrilegious, quite possibly all three together. Life is a serious, responsible business; we must do all that we can to avoid committing mortal sin and thus losing our souls. It is hard enough to keep all the rules and all the commandments, to live up to all our responsibilities. There isn't much time for celebration. Sex is a burden, an obligation, a necessity. How could that possibly be both the cause and an occasion for celebration?

Even in this allegedly post-Freudian age of permissiveness the "religious" argument is pretty much in the form I have presented it here. Its underlying assumption is that religion must be life-suspicious if not life-denying. Man is not a creature to be trusted; his instincts, his passions, his hungers are dubious and dangerous. He must be controlled, restrained, disciplined, held in check. That is, after all, what religion is all about.

It may be what some religions are all about, but it is not what biblical religion is all about. As Professor Walter Bruggemann of Eden Theological Seminary notes in his book, *In Man We Trust* (John Knox Press, 1972), "The wise in Israel characteristically appreciate life, love life, value it, and enjoy it. They appropriate the best learning, newest knowledge, and the most ingenious cultural achievements." Jesus told us that he came that we might have life and have it more abundantly. Even in the context of the New Testament that did not mean just life of the soul or life after death; it meant life for the human person, composite body and soul; life that would not end but life that would be more abundant now. Sex is part of life, the principle of life, the means by which life is continued. If Jesus came to bring us richer and more abundant life, then it is an inevitable consequence of his coming that our sex ought to be richer and more abundant. If it has not become so in the years that have elapsed since the appearance of Jesus, the fault is not in the brilliance or the clarity of his message but in our own fear and timidity and refusal to take him seriously, a refusal which consists essentially in not believing that when Jesus *said* "life" he *meant* life.

We do strain toward the transcendent, toward that which is beyond the here and now, beyond the confines of our segment of the time/space continuum. We do hunger for the absolute; we do seek that love which is eternally permanent. But we do not strain toward the absolute by running away from or denying or minimizing that love which exists to open up our personalities to a loving graciousness of the cosmos. A woman who thinks that she is obedient to the demands of absolute love when she restrains, restricts, and inhibits her passion for the man who shares her bed every night has a twisted notion at best of what love is and of what the graciousness is that Jesus revealed. A man whose relationship with his woman alternates between quick passion and silent shame may convince himself that this is a religious approach to the regrettably necessary filth of human sexuality, and he may do so in perfect good faith; but for all his good faith he thoroughly misunderstands that passionate God who reveals himself on Sinai, that Jesus who showed up at the marriage feast of Cana, and the religious implications of his wife's sexual attractiveness.

Both may argue that the life-suppressing or life-denying religious approach is what they were taught when they were growing up, and they may scapegoat "Catholic schools" for such teaching, implying that the schools deceived them and by this deceit dispensed them from modifying their attitudes in adult life. Heaven only knows that a lot of odd things were taught in Catholic schools, and that in its present manifestation Catholic Christianity is ill at ease with the life-affirming, life-endorsing themes of the Scripture—though in truth it is much less so than orthodox Protestantism. High level Catholic theory does indeed assert that human nature is basically trustworthy, and that while man may be "wounded," he is not basically flawed, much less depraved. High level theory even admits, grudgingly perhaps, that, despite the Augustinian tradition, the life-affirming, life-celebrating aspects of sexuality are good and wholesome and reflective and symbolic of God's passion for humankind. St. Augustine notwithstanding, the marriage rituals of the Catholic tradition down through the ages were simply unable to overlook the Cana dimension, that is to say, the celebratory aspect, of human sexual union.

The Protestant tradition, as Professor Bruggemann concedes, is much more suspicious of man, his life, his instincts, and his culture. But however strong the life-affirmation theories may have been in high-level Catholic theology, they filtered down erratically to the Sunday sermons, the catechisms, the textbooks, the marriage instructions. They grew badly confused in the endless controversy over what methods of family planning were appropriate—as though this were the only question of human sexuality on which the Catholic tradition could possibly shed any light. There were bits and pieces of teaching lying around from which many Catholics could, and some did, arrive at the correct conclusion that life is good and must be affirmed, that sex is admirable and must be celebrated. Such people enjoyed life and celebrated sex and paid rather little attention to what they read in the *Register* or the *Sunday Visitor* or heard from their parish priest on Sundays. Still, for most Catholic Christians it comes as a rude shock to be told that sex is a celebration and a Eucharist to be celebrated. The logic is obvious enough and the conclusion may not be altogether implausible, yet it is a surprise to hear it.

A man may thoroughly enjoy squeezing his wife's buttocks as he presses her body against his, but to be told that this is not only not sinful but religiously admirable and possessed of a hint of divine graciousness is disconcerting. He had some difficulty in persuading himself that such delight is not dirty, now he is told that it is religious celebration. That may be the case, he admits, but no one ever told him that before, and it is a definition of religion that he finds startling. Still, unless he is incorrigibly puritanical, he may find himself more than a little intrigued by such a religion.

And the woman who has sufficiently overcome the sexual fears instilled in her by her mother and by the nuns who taught her in high school to be able to gently reach for her husband's penis when she awakens sexually aroused in the middle of the night may be somewhat surprised when she is informed that such action is not "base" but a form of Eucharistic celebration, of ceremonial thanksgiving. Religion, as she remembers it, was a series of obligations dealing with things that one ought not to do and ought not to think. It was not a paradigm for festivity and celebration. Still a religion that comes down firmly on the side of more sex and better sex may not, after all, be a religion that she can write off as irrelevant.

But do either of these people really need a celebratory interpretive scheme to underwrite and reenforce their sexual life? The man does squeeze that soft and appealing area of his wife's anatomy, and she does reach for him in the middle of the night. Their biological urges, their human consequences and good taste, their affection for one another, their understanding of what it takes to keep a contemporary marriage alive and well have been sufficient for them to overcome their inhibitions, their fears, their guilts. They are capable of a fertile life, however hesitant and with whatever residues of past guilt feelings remain. Is a religion that tells them that these actions are Eucharist celebrations linked indeed in meaning and intention with the public celebration of the Eucharistic celebration that goes on in Church? What does that religion have to add to what is already occuring in their relationship?

There are, I think, three levels on which the question can be answered. A life-celebrating religious symbol system endorses and reinforces their sexual playfulness. It helps to sweep away the restraints, the fears, the inhibitions that may remain. Second, it encourages them to further exploration and growth together not only in their sex life but in all the dimensions and aspects of their common life together. Celebrations are self-regenerating. One good party deserves and demands another. One festive event leads us to want to plan another. Finally, and most important, a life-celebrating religion gives them the faith, the courage, and the hope they need to keep celebrating together when the going gets tough, and when the anti-life forces, which are still powerfully at work in the cosmos, threaten to drain the vitality, trust, and hope out of their relationship. One need not even see this religious contribution taking place only in times of difficulty and crisis. It has been a bad day for both husband and wife. They have not exactly quarreled, but resentments, angers, frustrations, bitterness have built up. Her bottom still looks attractive and squeezeable, but he is too angry to squeeze, and she is too angry to respond with anything but hostility. Yet if they believe in a passionately loving graciousness, whose goodness they celebrate in their common life together, each will lean towards graciousness to the other, and such a small difference can transform lives.

An explicit religious conviction about the graciousness of the deity and sex as a celebration of that graciousness may be a resource that is not absolutely indispensable for a happy common life and a playful sexual relationship, but it doesn't hurt. When the chips are really down, people fall back on their ultimate interpretive scheme, and then, almost inevitably, the man and woman who believe explicitly and consciously in life-affirming graciousness can survive together the worst of times.

It is possible, then, to accept and live by a world-view that affirms the goodness of life and of sexual union, and to believe that sex is celebration, Communion, Eucharist. Under such circumstances, a religious context of sexual playfulness exists not merely in the marriage ceremony but in the daily lives of husband and wife. However, this celebration is still essentially private. It is not shared with others, and it is not part of religious ceremony outside of family life. Is there any way that sexual playfulness can be deprivatized and resacralized in the public domain? Can one share one's celebration with others, while still keeping church and community from "messing" in one's private life? All one can do at this stage of the development of thought is raise the question. Perhaps in centuries to come our inability to think out an answer to the question will be viewed by our descendants as bizarre. Still, the transition from objective playfulness to subjective playfulness in human sexuality is an awkward one. It is perhaps our misfortune to live right in the middle of the transition.

Two points can be made as footnotes to the discussion. First, the custom is growing for groups of married couples (usually three or four) to go away for a weekend together. Unlike Bob and Carol, Ted and Alice, everybody keeps to his own marriage bed. There is eating and drinking, swimming and dancing, perhaps even skiing and hiking. There is also a lot of sex; indeed the whole purpose of the weekend is that the husband and wife can get away from the home and children for a brief interlude of sexual abandonment. While each couple is having its own private orgy and comment about it may be restrained (or not), there is little doubt that the communal context is seen as enhancing the fun and games that go on in the individual bedrooms. Such elegant balance between privacy and communality, between group support and group orgy, may not be everybody's cup of tea, but it does indicate, I think, that some people are wrestling with the problem of keeping their sex lives private and still sharing the happiness and joy of their sexuality with friends without resorting to the barbarism and foolishness of spouse-swapping.

There is also a tendency among some married people to ritualize or ceremonialize some of their lovemaking. Protocols of undressing, bathing, anointing, are deliberately and consciously followed to enhance the sexual relationship and to guarantee that lovemaking is, at least on some occasions, not a hasty, casual, almost thoughtless encounter. Again, such ceremonials will not appeal to everyone, and will seem to some to be foolish and kinky. But such attempts to receremonialize intercourse indicate that despite the matter-of-fact mechanistic rationality of most of the sex manuals, many people have come to understand that sex and love are mysteries, and it is much more effective to celebrate mysteries than to try to understand them.

Throughout most of the course of human history men and women have realized (though usually not self-consciously) that sex was a mystery to be celebrated—in addition to all the other things it was. To contemporary human beings that notion—so obvious to their predecessors—seems strange, unreal, and dubious. When a man and woman begin to investigate the possibilities of sex as celebration, they feel awkward and uneasy and even guilty. For Catholics, in particular, there is irony as well as poignancy in this guilt. They had to overcome a lot of guilt to take sex out of the moralistic context in which it was seen as a remedy to concupiscence and something which was not sinful for married people so long as they were ready to produce numbers of children. With considerable effort (and not always

with too much success) some Catholics are now
able to think of sex as a normal, natural, healthy,
expansive part of human life, and sexual playfulness as a desirable goal. Now they must overcome
exactly the opposite guilt and resacralize sex. It
is not merely a healthy, delightful, enjoyable part
of life; it is also a revelation, a sacrament, the
Eucharist, a participation in the basic life forces
of the universe. As such, it must be uninhibitedly,
wildly playful. For other Christians this transition has been spread over a couple of generations.
But Catholics have been playing "catch-up" ball
in recent decades and must cram many conflict-
ing experiences into one generation. Whether one
likes to have to shed two sets of guilt within one
lifetime or not depends upon how resourceful or
how playful one is or is willing to become. Some
people may find it a splendid opportunity.

chapter 7

Playing is serious, but it is not the same as that of the "real world." The game of play is the game of make-believe, though it is not unreal. It has a different sort of reality than can be found in our mundane existence. We can be very serious about our game and still not confuse it with what might be appropriate concern for a sick child, with the consideration of a professional opportunity, or a threat to the peace of the world. We play the game to win, of course. A rout or a triumph can have effects on our mundane existence. Still, one invalidates the game by equating success or failure in life with winning or losing the game. When one does that, the barriers between play and the ordinary world break down, and the rules of the game have been violated.

Games also tend to be both fun and funny. One rarely sees a professional football player laugh at himself when he drops a forward pass. The Roumanian tennis star who seemed to think that the Forest Hills tennis championship was a splendid joke was considered a bit bizarre. For those of us whose living does not depend on how well we perform on the athletic field, it is somewhat easier to laugh at mistakes. A mighty swing and the golf ball dribbles off the tee, an agile leap on water skis over a wave only to be caught by the next and tumbled into the water, a smashing overhand shot and the ball is missed by a foot—these are the breaks of the game, and at our best moments we can laugh at them. The one who laughs too quickly is not deeply involved in the game, and the one who refuses to laugh at all has become so involved that he can no longer be playful. Both have failed to achieve the proper balance of serious engagement.

Professional athletics has become so major a business enterprise that such whimsical free spirits as Johnny "Blood" McNally are no longer permitted to frolic on the frozen turf of Green Bay, Wisconsin, on a late autumn Sunday afternoon. A moderately bizarre character like Joe Kapp did not last very long; he was too erratic and unpredictable. But professional athletes make up for the fact that business has squeezed the playfulness out of their game by their endless jokes and laughter (frequently lubricated by quantities of post-game, post-season booze). Don Meredith was unable to laugh at the Dallas Cowboys' annual loss to the Green Bay Packers while he was playing, but now that he is a Monday-evening entertainer he manages to see the wry humor in what Green Bay did to him every season.

Play, then, can be funny. There is a strain toward hilarity in the world of play. The strain can be resisted, the hilarity eliminated but only at the risk of taking a great deal of the fun and pleasure out of the game. Sexual play is necessarily and inevitably funny. When a man and woman are not able to laugh with and at each other their relationship is certainly not playful. Laughter is both the cause and effect of playfulness in sex. It dispels strains, tensions, fears, and enables people to become playful.

That sex is funny does not need demonstration. It would appear that every culture the world has ever known has a tradition of "obscene" humor. Such humor is frequently crude, rude, and tasteless. It is also often cruel and exploitive, but it is also funny. Those who say that the dirty joke is "terrible" still manage to laugh at it. Neither theology nor social science has paid much attention to "obscene" humor. Theology has usually been content with denouncing the dirty joke as sinful, though conceding that among adults it is probably only a venial sin. Social science, when it pays any attention to the subject at all, usually does no more than footnote Freud's writing on wit and the unconscious. (One exception is the folklore collection, *Rationale of the Dirty Joke: An Analysis of Sexual Humor,* by G. Legman; Grove Press, 1968; a long, ponderous, and dreadfully dull encyclopedia of folk humor, which, for all its comprehensiveness, offers relatively little in the way of systematic interpretation.) One can't help but wonder what the reason is for such neglect. Everyone has heard dirty jokes; such a universal form of behavior must tell us something important about the human condition. Yet, it is swept under the rug. Surely in our permissive times the reason cannot be that people are afraid to discuss something as apparently trivial and base as obscene humor. That "permissiveness" of which we are so inordinately proud is dreadfully serious. There are many things we can show on a motion picture screen that we never could before, but sexual humor doesn't seem to be one of them. Indeed, the old bedroom farces of the '30s and '40s had a freedom to laugh about sex (without ever using the word) that our present heavy-handed cinematic protagonists of permissiveness do not seem to enjoy. One need only compare such dreadful and dour plays as *Hair* or *Oh! Calcutta* with the Restoration comedies to see the difference between serious sex and playful sex—and between exploitive fifth-rate art and creative talent. Puritanism persists in its illegitimate child, permissiveness. You can do just about anything you want with sex in contemporary America except laugh at it.

What is so funny about sex? The question must be answered on two levels. First, what are the aspects of human sexuality that trigger laughter? Secondly, why are we predisposed to respond with hilarity to sexual situations?

To begin with, the naked human body is funny. It may be radiantly beautiful, but it is also slightly ridiculous. A man or woman without clothes is caught in an embarrassing, absurd, awkward situation. We expect people to wear clothes, and when they don't it is a startling contrast. The dignity, the reserve, the aloofness, the coolness to which we pretend all slip away and we stand revealed in our alliance to the animal kingdom. All our fine pretensions to the abstract, theoretical, etherealized spirit dissolve in a cold blast of air on our goose-bumped bodies.

In our culture, where men are supposed to be far more interested in sex than women, part of the fun for a man in conquering a woman is to get her clothes off so that she stands revealed as being every bit as much a sexual being as he is. She may primly pretend not to be interested in sex, or not to be capable of sexual arousal, or to be able to suppress her sexual instincts; but get her clothes off and all that pretense is gone. Destroying pretense is, of course, a very laughter-provoking phenomenon in human culture. The drunk who pretends to be in complete control falls flat on his face and the crowd roars. The woman who pretends to be a sexless creature (at least relative to the superior sexuality of the man) loses her clothes and is revealed as thoroughly sexual after all. Her man laughs, although, if he is wise, only to himself.

In other cultures, where the woman is presumed to be the more highly sexed, it is very likely that the exact opposite phenomenon occurs. Even in our own culture a self-possessed woman with a sense of humor and a willingness to speak honestly about her reactions will admit that there is something mutually amusing in catching a man by surprise without his clothes on. His male dignity and his pretense at masculine superiority are snatched away from him, and he stands revealed as a creature who is hesitant and uncertain about his sexual nature as is any woman. He reaches quickly for his clothes, his mask of male aloofness, but still he has been caught, found out, revealed; and the contrast between pretense and reality is laugh-provoking.

Laughter at the body of another can be cruel, particularly when it is a means of self-defense. But it need not be cruel. We can laugh at another body stripped of its clothes and pretenses with tenderness and affection. To the somber and the serious, it seems quite impossible to laugh at what one loves and finds beautiful, but one need only think of the laughter of parents at their children to realize how amusement, respect, affection, love can all be combined. The parent finds the child precious, important, beautiful, and also funny. One laughs at the little thing as he tries, oh so seriously and oh so awkwardly, to take his first steps across the room. He is beautiful, admirable, touching, and so funny; and these characteristics are so inextricably linked that we cannot separate them, and no one should bother to try.

So we love the body of our sexual partner and admire it and take pleasure in it and laugh at it because it is simultaneously beautiful, desirable, and funny. Any attempt to exclude one of these responses from the web of our reaction makes that reaction stunted and incomplete.

But if nakedness is funny, sexual arousal is even funnier. (As much of the wit of "obscene" humor understands.) We are curiously proud creatures, animal to be sure, but animals with a difference. We make elaborate pretenses at being superior to our fellow creatures (which we surely are) to such a degree that we are scarcely animal at all. We are self-disciplined, self-controlled, the master of our own emotions and our own destiny. We are the only animal that walks upright and even our simian relatives scurry along the ground on all fours very often. We can't do that any more, and our upright stance is the symbol of our evolutionary superiority. We only need two limbs to move about, and we can thereby use the other two for implementing and executing the ingenious design our brains laid out for us. A superior creature in-

deed is humankind; his intellect controls and
dominates everything he does. Other creatures
are slaves to their instincts and their responses.
Humankind creates his own meaning systems and
then organizes the phenomena of life to fit these
experiences. He has come down out of the trees,
moved out of the forest, and walks through the
fields and the streets of his cities on his hind legs.
The Lord of Creation he unquestionably is.

But when he (or she) is sexually aroused much
of that evolutionary superiority slips away. Unlike the reproductive interludes of other animals,
those of human beings are fraught with meaning.
They are self-conscious, self-reflective, self-
defining acts. Still, they are fierce animal actions
in which much of the self-control, self-discipline,
and self-possession slips away. It is simply impossible to be in the full heat of sexual arousal
and pretend that one is playing it cool and that one
is immune to the power of fierce, non-rational
forces. The contrast between the pose of complete
self-possession, which humankind maintains most
of the time, and fierce animal desire, which dominates the sexual encounter, is extremely funny—
if not to the aroused person himself then at least
to those who are watching him through the prism
of a dirty joke. Part of the fun of teasing one's
sexual partner certainly involves delight in making him ever so slightly ludicrous. As one's
partner becomes aroused he is transformed from
self-control and self-possession to passionate

hunger. That transformation is amusing to those who are sophisticated enough to enjoy it. Sexual partners can do funny things to one another; they can tease, distract, take over the imagination, cause odd and peculiar transformations in the shape, the rhythm, the color, and even smell of the other body. In the process, the defenses, the dignity, and the self-possession of the other slip away, and he (or she) does indeed become rather like an amusing, desirable, lovable child taking his first stroll from chair to coffee table.

We lose our dignity in sexual encounters. While lovemaking ought to be elegant, it can certainly never be dignified or solemn the way other important events in our lives are. There is too much emotion, too much power, too much uncontrollable response, too much automatic and violent physical response for us to maintain poses when we are making love. One of the reasons why lovemaking is in most societies done privately is simply that so much dignity is lost that we would be embarrassed to have others see what wild animals we become in sexual exchange.

Furthermore, most human activities are carried on in an upright stance. Lovemaking, despite Marlon Brando, usually occurs in ungainly, awkward, uncomfortable, and slightly ridiculous positions. The postures required to bring together the sexual organs of a man and a woman are very far from a beautifully choreographed ballet. The dignity of a creature who fancies himself mostly spirit and only inconsequentially animal is thrust away as he is gripped by the raw passions of his animal nature. Humans look ridiculous as they make love only because of the contrast between their amorous thrashings and the dignity and self-control that mark their upright life is so dramatic. Sex is funny because it so devastatingly reminds us that we are both animal and spirit, and the pretense of the spirit to be free of and secure in its domination of the animal is at best a risky and tenuous position.

The richest, the most powerful, the most influential man in the world is reduced to the common denominator of our animal condition when he is sexually aroused, and the most aristocratic, refined, elegant woman is no different from any other woman when a man's body is united with hers. It is the capacity of human sexuality to bring everyone down to the same common denominator of our fundamental animal nature. There may be great pleasure in lying flat on one's back stark naked, one's legs spread apart, while someone else's body enters one's own; but there is no refinement, no daintiness, no self-possession at all in such a posture. There may also be great pleasure in mounting and plunging into the body which is now being possessed, but it is not pretty. They engage in their coupling in private partially because they know that what they are doing is in startling contrast to the way they normally behave and that others might find that contrast very funny.

When a man and woman make love to one another they also temporarily make fools out of themselves. They may suppress this fact and pretend that what they are doing is serious, sober, and dreadfully important. When this pretense is maintained in the face of almost overwhelming evidence to the contrary, the relationship between the man and woman offers the raw material for much of the high comedy the human race has produced. The intercourse interlude within such a relationship is responsible for almost all of our low comedy. Funny things happen when a man and woman make love to one another. They can pretend that it's not hilarious and thus protect their fragile egos, but such a pretense misses much of what goes on in the situation and absolutely precludes the possibility of sex's being playful.

One can laugh at oneself and one's sexual partner only in a context of a basically secure relationship. For laughter heals; it does not hurt. The little child trying to walk does not mind his parents' laughter, because he assumes that laughter and love are not inconsistent, and that laughter is simply another manifestation of love. If the husband and wife have developed a style in their marriage in which one is free to laugh because it is perceived as supportive and affectionate, then they will find it hard to control that laughter when they are having sex together. But if their relationship is heavy, somber, serious, responsible, then there is simply no way that they can begin to find anything amusing when the bedroom door is closed and their clothes are removed. When everything seems to be riding on the maximum amount of pleasure and success from this particular sexual encounter, the whole affair loses its humor entirely—which is, of course, a problem not only with serious marriages but with affairs that are too serious to be laughed at and hence too serious to be playful.

A man and woman who are close to one another develop a whole private agenda of shared jokes, frequently shared in a code that is only understood by the two of them. A shared joke becomes even funnier if it is a secret one. This secret agenda of shared laughter may include hilarious experiences in the whole of their common life, including those that occurred in bed. No couple's agenda of shared wit will be just like any other couple's; no one can prescribe for others what they will find funny (though heaven knows some sex manuals try). Private jokes are private jokes; by definition they can be imposed by no one else.

One couple, for example, goes into uncontrollable laughter whenever someone else uses the word "plunger." Their friends don't exactly understand what they are laughing at, and think it best not to ask. However, one night after the "creetur" had flowed liberally, the couple told their friends why that word was so funny. For reasons that they couldn't explain the two of them found the "plopping" sound made when the husband's sweat-soaked body pulled off the wife's breasts, to which he had become "glued" during lovemaking, to be an incredibly funny phenomenon. It sounded so much like the noise of a plunger cleaning a drain that they began to call this aspect of their lovemaking "the plunger effect." It invariably brought their sex exchange to an end in peals of laughter.

Others might not even notice such an experience, might not think it particularly funny, and certainly would not look forward to it as a pleasant bit of frosting on the cake. But what others might think makes no difference. For this particular couple this quite ordinary and trivial sound has become a shared joke, a shared delight, and a pleasant bit of their comic game, a game that was *theirs* and no one else's.

We only share jokes with our friends. Indeed, we normally only tell dirty jokes to those we are sure will let us get away with it. Hence we can appreciate the humor, the wit, the incongruity, the foolishness of our sexuality only when it is shared with a close friend. Casual, transient sex simply cannot be funny, because the background of common experience, the pre-existing agenda of shared jokes into which the laughter of this particular interlude can be fit, is not there. Transient sex is necessarily serious. We are afraid of laughter because we assume, usually correctly, that it will be interpreted as hurting rather than healing laughter. Only after a sustained relationship has been built can we be sure that our partner is laughing with us and not at us.

At a deeper level, laughter serves to reduce aggression and reduce fear. Psychiatrists agree that laughter is a form of aggression, but it need not hurt nor be intended to hurt. It communicates something that is important and demanding but with the barb removed or blunted. If we are angry at someone else we can get rid of it by losing our temper or by diverting it into laughter, which simultaneously releases the angry energies and enriches and enhances the relationship. Laughter is a safety-valve that enables us to get a perspective on our own aggressive emotions and share them with the other in a way he can accept and deal with. Two people who live together in the oppressive intimacy of a sustained sexual union will either develop a way of communicating much of their aggressions through the soft language of laughter, or they will repress the aggression, or they will tear one another apart. Laughter is obviously the most attractive of the three alternatives.

But above all laughter dispels fear. It is, as Peter Berger points out in his *A Rumor of Angels,* a blunt assertion from humankind that it is not afraid even of death. All laughter is a laughing at death, according to Berger, and at those fears and anxieties which are ultimately rooted in death.

Sex is a scary business, which explains why so many of the psychological disturbances that afflict humankind are sexual either in their origins or their manifestations or both. In sex we put ourselves on the line both physically and psychologically in a way we do in practically no other kind of activity. (Public speaking is another and related form of self-exposure that evokes related forms of terror and delight.) The confident, supreme, certain lover is a faker, who cannot admit to himself or anyone else that he shares the common lot of humankind, that he too is afraid of sex. The theologian John Dunne in his book *Time and Myth* (Doubleday, 1973) suggests that fear of sexuality is linked to our primal fear of death: "Sexuality is not only fascinating but dreadful, it seems, for it is experienced as a terrible purpose at work in one's life, a purpose that is not personal but somehow impersonal in its themes, a purpose that looks to the species rather than the individual, to the reproduction of one's kind rather than to one's own personal development. If we were to ask, 'Why do we fear our sexuality?' we would undoubtedly be told that we fear it because we have been taught to fear it, because we have learned to see it as fraught with moral danger. In reality, though, the fear seems to go well beyond merely learned fears. It is like the fear of death. We could be told also that we have been taught to fear death, that we fear it because we have learned to fear it. Yet death seems in fact to be inherently fearful. Actually, we fear both our sexuality and our mortality for the same reason, it seems, because they are forces within us that drive beyond all personal goals, that threaten our personal existence by leading beyond it."

If Dunne is right, and it seems to me that he is, then the naive notion, so popular in our time, that we can stop being afraid of sex if we can get rid of the silly and ignorant fears we acquired from our family, our schools, our churches is a foolish self-deception. The goal of "sex without fear" is a false one, and energies wasted on it are invested in self-deception. It would be much better to deal with sexual fear by not denying it or writing it off as a residue of an unenlightened past, but by respecting it, understanding it, coping with it, and transcending it.

A man and woman locked in a sustained relationship with each other are crazy if they do not acknowledge that there is fear in that relationship. The other is so close, knows one so well, and has so much power and influence over one. Ridicule, betrayal, infidelity can break a heart, and the other has the power to use them if he (or she) chooses. There is pleasure in being afraid of that other and in acknowledging it. Indeed it may be possible to engage in playfulness only when that fear is out in the open and can be laughed at together.

Laughter in sex, then, is a response to fear, and the ultimate origins of sexual humor can be found, I suspect, in our fear of the awesome power of sex, a power, as Father Dunne points out, that draws our life out beyond ourself. We laugh at death and we laugh at sex because if we don't laugh at them they may well overwhelm us. We laugh also because of the stubborn conviction, irresistibly present in the depths of our personalities, that in the long run we will have the last laugh at the terrors of death and at the terrors of sex. They both may draw us out beyond our own personal existence, and when we get out there we stubbornly believe, at least part of the time, that what we feared turns out not to be fearsome at all.

So lovers laugh together at themselves and at one another because they are afraid of the power of their sexuality, because they are afraid of one another, but also because they are convinced that they can transcend the fear and find out that their sexuality and their sexual fears are even more delightful than they are terrifying. That delight conquers terror is a basic and fundamental human religious hope. It is a hope, incidentally, that Jesus came into the world to confirm. The revelation of God's love as grounds for hope stands as solid reinforcement for the uncontrollable laughter of true lovers who are swept away by the delights they experience in playing with one another.

But if laughter is a response to fear, indeed, the only effective response, it is also severely inhibited by fear. We are afraid to laugh. Our sexuality and our sexual union are serious and important matters. Much of our life happiness will depend upon them; they are not matters to be taken lightly. Therefore it seems inappropriate, almost blasphemous, to laugh. Sex is horrifying, shameful, vile, base, depraved, on the one hand; but on the other, sexual orgasm is absolutely indispensable for self-fulfillment and to prove our masculinity or our femininity and to keep a marriage together. To the puritan and the hedonist, sex is surely not a laughing matter.

It is a strong possibility that sex without humor becomes cruel. For either we release our aggressions and dispel our fears with laughter or we protect ourselves from what the other may do to us. Cruelty is one of the best forms of self-protection that the twisted human psyche has ever produced. It is hard not to laugh at the awkward, ungainly, undignified interlude of sexual encounter, but we can repress it; we can make the event somber, serious, and most people manage to do it most of the time. Fear doesn't go away, of course, but it does get repressed, and then seeps out in vengeful, destructive, and punitive disguises. Instead of sex being too important to laugh at, it is too important not to laugh at.

Life is a mixture of comedy and tragedy. We deny the existence of one or the other only at the risk of deceiving ourselves. The basic question is not whether we can dispense with either comedy or tragedy but whether comedy might just not possibly be ever-so-slightly more powerful than tragedy. Sex, the fundamental life-giving power, reflects the ambiguity of life. It is both terror and delight. If we believe that delight is ever-so-slightly more important than the terror, then we are free to laugh. But, paradoxically, in our freedom to laugh we discover that the power of delight exorcises terror. The husband and wife who share the crude little joke about the "plunger effect" may have many problems in their relationship. It is unlikely that fear has been completely eliminated from their sexual life (it can never happen in this world), but they do have a joke they share. When anger, hatred, or fear threatens to disrupt the playfulness of their union, there is always the joke to help dispel these enemies. If their intelligence is sophisticated they will not deny the fear involved in their sex, for if sex is not something important and powerful enough to be afraid of, then it is likely to be uninteresting and dull. But their joke and the context of humor and play that surrounds it will help keep fear at bay. Whether their joke is a reflection of a great Cosmic Joke in which life successfully puts down death remains to be seen. It is not necessary that they see their "plunger effect" as a reflection of the Cosmic Joke, but it won't hurt them if they do.

chapter 8

From one perspective playful sexuality seems to be the easiest thing in the world. Playfulness is built into the psychological and physiological dynamics of the situation. It is hard for sex not to be festive, fantastic, humorous. A man and woman should develop patterns of playing together which are as easy and as natural as an apple falling off a tree. But in fact we know that relatively few couples do indeed develop such patterns of playfulness. Many will even argue that playfulness is a romantic, sentimental, idealistic illusion. Temptations against playfulness must be strong indeed if they are able to overcome what seems to be an almost natural propensity.

Let us take several examples of relatively minor sexual playfulness.

It is a summer afternoon. The husband is drowsing on the couch, the children are outside playing. The wife comes up to the couch, runs her fingers through his hair, and as he awakens from his nap, she begins to gently kiss him—his eyes, nose, ears, forehead, lips, chin. The kisses are at first bare touches, but the strength and power of them build up. She concludes with an extremely passionate, lingering, inviting, overwhelmingly suggestive kiss on his lips. At that point she leaves quickly for the yard, leaving him very much awake.

The man comes home from work just as his wife is getting out of the shower. He takes the towel from her hands and begins to dry her off. She protests at first that she must get dinner ready. But then, as he briskly and competently moves the towel over her body she accepts his ministrations docilely, her eyes growing wider with pleasure and anticipation. He pats her derriere and tells her to get on with the business of dinner.

The husband is on the telephone for what is a long and important call. His wife comes up behind him, puts her arms around him and squeezes hard. She then begins to gently nibble on the back of his neck, distracting him from his phone call. He doesn't seem to mind enough to push her away, but just as the call is coming to an end she leaves him to busy herself with something else.

Husband and wife are in the back of a car going somewhere with friends. The husband's hand creeps under her skirt and moves slowly up her thigh. She makes a face and tries, not too convincingly, to push him away. His hand continues its exploration of the sensitive areas, and when they arrive at the party his wife has many other things on her mind.

The two of them are in the front seat of their own car in stop-and-go traffic. The husband's driving is frustrated and impatient. His wife's hand, which was resting on his arm, seeks another area of his body, and the husband finds his waiting for the traffic to move substantially more easy to bear.

Guests are due in five minutes. The wife is putting on finishing touches in front of the mirror. The husband walks by and suddenly finds his wife's back extremely attractive. He deftly unhooks her bra, squeezes her breasts against her body, covers her back with kisses, and murmurs passionately what a beautiful woman she is. The interlude lasts but a minute; the doorbell rings, and the guests begin to arrive.

A number of things are to be noted about all of these incidents. They are utterly trivial and commonplace. They are minor in the sense that they require little activity and not much in the way of immediate response. They are gratuitous in that they are easy to do, make almost no demands on time, and run no risk of shocking children. (Would children be shocked to find their mother kissing their father? One hopes not!) They interfere not in the least with serious obligations and responsibilities. They are supportive, euphoric, quite unnecessary, spontaneous, simple, easy. In a way it is almost hard not to do them. Such actions, or at least those like them, are simply manifestations of spontaneous, natural, impulsive, propensities of sexually healthy men and women living in close proximity to each other. A squeeze, a touch, a kiss, a caress, a nibble, a period of exploration—there are few things in life that can be done more cheaply or easily. They are quintessentially playful.

They are jokes, tricks, games, teases. They are exercises in fantasy and minor tidbits of festivity. In such situations the inclination to indulge in such playfulness is very strong. It is what virtually everyone would like to do in such circumstances, and yet what very few manage to do.

The opportunities are there; the payoff is evident; the procedure is clear; and still nothing happens. Are there sexual hang-ups? Probably. But the real problem goes deeper than sexuality. If a man and woman, pushed together in the intimacy of their common life, cannot or do not respond the way their spontaneous impulses incline them, the flaw in their personalities and their relationship is human rather than only sexual.

Before they came together they fantasized a life that would be filled with certain spontaneous exchanges of affection, enticement, and encouragement. But they somehow never got started, or, perhaps, they have long since stopped what began so tentatively and never developed. In their day-dream relationship they may act like tender, playful lovers; but in the real world they share together, playfulness and affection are restrained, inhibited, and repressed. If they are asked why, they might respond that other things are more important than sex in their life together, or that they have so many commitments, responsibilities, or distractions, or that sex just isn't so important as it used to be, or that we could hardly expect them to act like children or adolescents.

All of these answers may be true. The adjustment they have worked out together may be a satisfactory one, on the whole, for both of them. No one can seize all the opportunities in life, and if two people choose to focus on other opportunities that they think are incompatible with sexual playfulness, then that is their decision. But I must raise the question whether their whole existence might not be constrained, cautious, conservative, careful, and that a constricted sexuality is merely the reflection of a constricted adjustment to life. May not their fundamental lifestyle be a "no"? No to possibility, no to risk, no to delight, no to reward. May they not have turned away from the opportunity of playfulness because their fundamental response to everything in life is a turning away from opportunity?

I must admit that my two decades of working

with young people have made me very melancholy about humankind in its present state of development. The lives of most of the young people I watched grow up are lives of easy opportunities needlessly lost. Their marriages and sexual relationships are just the most acute and obvious symbol of "no" that is said to all the opportunities of their lives. They are cautious, conservative, cynical not at thirty-five or forty but already at twenty-five, and some are that way at seventeen and eighteen. The great outburst of student activism in the '60s (itself a badly flawed and extremely deceptive phenomenon) blinded us to the fact that the young of today are even more cautious and conservative than their Depression-born parents. I do not know how one goes about preparing people to seize easy opportunities, particularly when the basic system that filtered to them through their parents and was reinforced by their teachers and clergy led them to believe that life is dangerous, punitive, repressive, and that the wise person takes no risks at all. Poets, novelists, political leaders, mystics, scholars, saints have all gone down the drain of cynicism and caution. Who in their right mind would expect such people to be playful lovers?

Their lives are filled with fear, anger, shame, dullness, cowardice, routine, monotony. They protect themselves from risk and punish those closest to them because they dared to threaten the thick armor-plating of self-sufficiency, which they used to protect their frail, frightened egos.

Married couples pile up vast quantities of anger and hatred towards one another in a life together. Not infrequently it becomes more important to punish, to inflict pain on the other, than to do anything else in life. It is all done implicitly, subtly, indirectly—though when the two have had enough to drink at a party, it is likely that the pain will burst out into the open. One resists the impulse to play with the other because the other might like the experience, and to deprive him or her of such pleasure is just about the only really meaningful reward left in life.

The wife passes by the husband dozing on the couch and the thought of teasing him with her kisses rises spontaneously in her imagination, but "kiss the son of a bitch? He should be out mowing the lawn."

The husband glances into the mirror and sees his wife combing her hair. The impulse to squeeze her and to tell her how yummy she looks is very strong, but he doesn't like the guests she invited and is not about to reward or encourage her before a party that is bound to be a drag. Punishment in both cases is more important than pleasure.

This may not be exactly the totality of the human condition, but unfortunately it is the way a very considerable number of people freely choose to live. It is easier to say "no" than to say "yes" to life. Once you affirm life, you deprive yourself of a very considerable capacity to inflict pain and suffering on those you hate (or love).

Father Dunne, in *Time and Myth* notes that we miss the whole point of James Joyce's *Ulysses* if we think it is merely about adultery in Dublin. For Ulysses has returned to Penelope, and we have here not merely twentieth-century Dublin but a classical, mythological theme and a fundamental human existential question. Does one say "yes" or "no" to the possibilities of life? At the mythological level the two lovers are saying "yes."

> I asked him with my eyes to ask again yes, and then he asked me would I say yes, to say yes, my mountain flower, and first I put my arms around him, yes, and drew him down to me so he could feel my breasts all perfume, yes, and his heart was going like mad, and yes I said yes I will, Yes.

Think what we will about Joyce and the characters who inhabited Dublin at the beginning of the century, the question of "yes" or "no" is not only sexual; it is the most basic and fundamental human and religious question that can be asked. Does one want to live fully or cautiously? Does one wish to be open or constricted, risk-taking or cynical? Playful people have playful sex, and their sexual playfulness reinforces and strengthens their playfulness as people. We become playful people only when we say "yes" to the opportunities that the Spirit of Life, with implacable insistence, offers us every day. For most people, the sexual partner to whom they are committed in a sustained relationship is the biggest single opportunity they will ever receive. It is the decisive opportunity, and whether they say "yes" or "no" will shape everything else that happens in their lives. If they say "no" they might just as well subscribe to *Playboy* or *Playgirl* because that is as close to playful sex as they will ever get.

chapter 9

I am surprised by the durability of puritanism. It may be that I am more a victim of the folklore about permissiveness and sexual revolution and hedonism than I had thought. I wrote my earlier book, *Sexual Intimacy*, more or less by accident in response to a request for a pamphlet. After a couple of decades of pre-Cana and Cana conferences and the second Vatican Council, the confusion of Freudian psychology, and the relaxation of many of the more rigid sexual taboos of years gone by, I would have thought that puritanism would be in full retreat. One could write, it seemed to me, a very frank book about human sexuality as an occasion for religious reflection on the meaning of sexuality. One need no longer be reticent about discussing the human body and its functions, about referring to sexual organs by their proper names, reflecting on the function of nudity and clothing on eroticism, and the development of a personal eroticism without having to fear the reaction. It turned out, however, that I had underestimated the strength of puritanism.

The puritanical response to *Sexual Intimacy* represented much less than the majority of those who wrote, but what astonished me about my puritanical correspondents was not that they disagreed with my approach but the vile, angry, hate-filled style of their disagreement. The puritan writers did not even bother to try to understand what was being said. The context of a chapter or of the whole book was irrelevant. Certain words had been mentioned, certain images had been suggested, certain practices described (for reasons that escape me, nude bathing, which I clearly disapproved of, was fiercely denounced), and that was enough to drive some letter writers to paroxysms of fierce anger.

As the man says, they do protest too much. They reveal more of their own unconscious and their own fantasy life than they could possibly imagine.

I was naive, of course. Puritanism is a remarkably strong element in human culture, and it will take a good deal more than a few half-baked and shallow "sexual revolutions" to sweep it aside. One cannot argue with a puritan, and I shall attempt to do no more of it in this book than I did in its predecessor. But the real problem is the tendency toward puritanism that exists in all of us; it is a dimension of practically all human beings that antedates Christianity. It managed to grip the early Christian religion in its clammy paws and took on Christian colors, the fakery and gaudiness of which have only recently become obvious to a few Christians. Puritanism is the ultimate sexual temptation, and in a way it is the ultimate human temptation. It is a decisive "no" to human sexuality, a decisive "no" to human goodness, a decisive "no" to the Gracious Vitality of the universe.

Puritanism is fundamentally a fear of sexuality. The puritan quite correctly notes that sex is dangerous simply because it cannot always be dominated by human rationality; it breaks out in wild, passionate, uncontrolled feelings and actions. It threatens chaos, so it must be evil, and the less we have to do with it the better off we will be. The Platonists, the Manichees, the Gnostics, all the ancient spiritualist heresies believed that man was Spirit, that the body imprisoned man, and that human sexuality, so obviously and painfully a function of the body, was the worst of the demons that bound and caged the human Spirit. More primitive peoples were superstitious in their fears of sexuality. They knew what sexual arousal could do to a warrior; it could deprive him of his will to fight. It knew that a sexually aroused woman was insatiable. It knew that sexuality kept the tribe in

existence, but it also recognized that it could unleash forces that could tear the tribe asunder. The
forces of sexuality had to be disciplined, controlled, restrained; and so an elaborate system of
taboos was set up to keep this fearsome power
under control. The Israelite religion was more
relaxed on the subject of sexuality than either the
nature religions or the Near Eastern heresies that
were platonic in inspiration. Still the Hebrews did
hedge sexuality in with an elaborate set of rituals
and stipulations. They remembered the fertility
goddesses their ancestors had fought in the hill
shrines of Palestine, and while now fertility was
seen as the dutiful servant of Yahweh, the Israel-
ites were not about to take chances.

The recognition of human weakness, which is
strong in St. Paul, stronger still in St. Augustine,
and very strong indeed in the Lutheran and classical reformers, provided a perfect opening for
puritanism to creep in and almost take possession
of Christianity. For more than a millennium-and-
a-half few if any Christian theologians had much
of a kind word to say about sexuality—despite the
sexual imagery that can be found in many different
places in the Scripture. (Jeremiah, Ezekial, Hosea
in the Old Testament and the gospels and epistles
in the New.) The puritans have had things all their
own way in the theory of human sexuality (save
in the marriage rituals and ceremonials). Indeed,
in the minds of many Christians, and particularly

Catholic Christians, the puritan style is indistinguishable from the Christian style. Sex is base, vile, dirty, shameful; it ought not to be discussed. It is basically a means for satisfying concupiscence and reproducing the human race.

Christianity is now in the process (under substantial prodding from the Freudians) of exorcising puritanism from the Christian tradition. It will not be an easy task. Puritanism survived as long as it has because it turns out to be a useful shield under which fear can hide.

Sex is demonic, make no mistake about it. It does unleash fierce and not altogether controllable powers in the human personality. It is ecstatic; it snatches human beings out of their ordinary modes of existence. Anything that is ecstatic and demonic must be approached with some caution and reserve. Fear of human sexuality seems to be built into the human condition, and it is a good thing to be afraid of it. The naive optimist who thinks that sexuality is something nice, neat, and natural, making no problems for anybody once they have shed all their "hang-ups," is kidding himself. There is a dark side to sex as well as a bright side, a destructive dimension as well as a constructive one. The wise person respects the demonic and the ecstatic elements of his sexuality. They can get him into trouble. They can make him do things that are hurtful to both him and others. Like all creative powers sexuality must be treated with some caution, some restraint and care. Such a viewpoint—offensive perhaps to encounter group hedonism—is sensible, discreet, wise.

But it doesn't go far enough for the puritan. It is not merely enough for him to caution about sex, one must also pronounce a condemnation of it. It is not enough to say that nothing excuses man from an exercise of rationality. Sex is not only nonrational, it is irrational. The rational man will have as little to do with it as possible.

One does not go nearly as far as the puritan wants when one says that sex is demonic; it must also be added that it is diabolic. One does not satisfy the puritan when one says that sex is ecstatic; it must also be said that it is evil. The puritan does not want to hear that we should have a healthy respect for the power of sexuality to get us into trouble. What he wants to hear is a simple statement that sex will always get us into trouble. When he is told that sexuality shapes human dignity because it reasserts the fundamental animal component of our personality, he is delighted. Animality is base, low, and wrong. When we act "like animals" we stop being human, which is, of course, evil. When we contend that sexuality is a complex, intricate problem that no one ever understands perfectly, he agrees with us and adds that the best way to cope with the problem is to have as little to do with it as possible.

And there is the essence of the puritan response. If you wish to avoid the danger, the difficulty, and the complexity of human sexuality condemn it and then try to stop sexual activity. It would be nice, the puritan admits, if people could be trusted with their animality, their sexuality, their passions; but obviously you can't trust them. So the best thing to do is to tell them that their passions are bad and that they should enjoy them as little as possible. That way we will protect people from the difficulty of making decisions, from the awesome responsibility of balancing passion and rationality. Life, the puritan argues, may not be quite as much fun if you accept his perspective, but it's a lot safer.

The puritan won't admit it, but sexuality, like all the other nonrational forces that sweep through the universe and inundate the human personality, is a trap, a temptation, a trick that an arbitrary, cantankerous, suspicious God is playing on humankind to see if we are smart and brave and tough enough to resist the temptation and avoid the dangers into which we are being tricked.

It is an interesting view of God, a not uncommon one in Christian and Catholic circles (the old Irish monsignor image of God). It has relatively little to do with the Yahweh of Sinai or the Jesus of Cana, but if the puritans are right and God is of the sort they say he is instead of the sort Jesus says he is, then we had better be pretty damn careful. For the Holy Spirit is not a benign trickster then, a playful imp, a poltergeist, a laughing spirit, a leprechaun; he is a mean, vindictive character who is abroad in the cosmos to trip us up, make fools of us, and send us off to hell if he possibly can. In the puritan world-view, the Holy Spirit seems quite indistinguishable from Satan. Hence it is understandable that that which is demonic (and of the Spirit) must also be seen as diabolic.

Puritanism comes to terms with the fearfulness of the cosmos of life and of sexuality by running from it. One either laughs or runs; the puritan says: "Run while you can. Run for your life!"

Puritanism is a religious world-view. It doesn't happen to be a Christian world-view, but it is religious; and within its own framework it is a consistent, serious, and devout religion. But it also turns out to be a very useful religion for underwriting no-saying. Indeed it turns "no" into an act of highest virtue. It is a defense against the attractiveness of others, a defense against the out-going dimensions of our own personality. It is a defense against the consuming demand to come forth that we hear from within ourselves and from some other or Other, who seems to be calling to us from Out There. Puritanism tells us that our safe, cynical, life-denying propensities, which we would like to indulge anyhow, represent the highest of human virtues. Do you want to be good? Fine. Deny life, deny love, deny risk, deny pleasure, deny delight. Just as the hedonist says, "enjoy, enjoy;" and the guilt-ridden liberal says, "expiate, expiate;" the puritan says, "deny, deny."

Puritanism has another use. It's a marvelous way of hating and punishing other human beings under the guise of virtue. We obtain strong ego-reinforcement by identifying with the cause of righteousness and virtue and by being shocked and outraged by all the immorality that swirls around. There is a curious lack of consistency and pattern in this sense of outrage. A pinup picture and a full-blown Reubens, a dirty joke and a scanty swimming suit, *Ulysses* and hard-core pornography, young people kissing in a car and rape—all merit equally violent outrage from the puritan. By donning the mantle of goodness and virtue the puritan can be as nasty, as vicious, as vindictive and as punitive as he wants. Everything he does, he argues, is done to protect virtue and morality.

The puritan is likely to be married, and as such he will occasionally "have sex." It is not important in his marriage, he will insist. He and his spouse love each other; they share many things in common, of which sex is only a relatively minor part. The principal joy in his marriage is his children, and he must do all he can to protect the morals of his children from corruption. (So off to the neighborhood drugstore to censor the magazine rack.) Sex is a burden that one must live with, but it ought not to be discussed or mentioned and only enjoyed in the strictest moderation. The very idea that sex should be playful strikes him as blasphemous. Or, as one puritan commented to me, "The Church was much better in the past when we never heard a thing about sex."

But for the puritan it is not enough that he drain the enjoyment out of his own sexuality; it is necessary for others to deny the enjoyment of theirs. Playfulness is not something to be renounced because of one's own taste; it is something to be denounced in others as fundamentally immoral and irresponsible. Horror, shock, dismay, anger—these are the stock in trade of the puritan when he hears the faintest suggestion that for other people sex might be fun.

And if the puritan happens to be married to someone less puritanical then the other is in deep trouble. The slightest hint that sexual pleasure and playfulness might be expanded is greeted with absolute horror and outraged harshness. "Don't you even think of anything like that ever again!" This is the puritan's response to the most harmless sexual innovation. It's bad enough for one to "have sex," but to make it frivolous or foolish or festive or fantastic is simply inviting the heavens to call down their outraged puritanical punishments on people who could be so vile.

What can one do with a puritan? Not much, I fear. The puritan has made his religion so much a part of his world-view and his personality that you can neither argue with him nor seduce him out of it. The person who is a self-conscious, principled puritan is incorrigible. Others may be reluctant puritans, trapped by their childhood experiences and their education into puritan attitudes and habits that they don't like and from which their intelligence tells them they ought to escape. Such reluctant puritans are enough to try the patience of a saint, and those of us who have to deal with them often have an impulse to shake them until they come to their senses. Gentleness, kindness, patience, persistence—and not infrequently psychotherapy—may help to liberate them. When there is a marriage between two such reluctant puritans (and in contemporary Catholicism, alas, such matches are all too frequent) one is presented with a very difficult relationship indeed. The prognosis must certainly be guarded; still, as the Scripture says, with God all things are possible. (And be it noted that in this context the Scripture is talking about getting a camel through the eye of a needle.)

I am not sure that a thoroughgoing, convinced puritan is really capable of marriage. The canon lawyers will probably have to figure this out (and they may get to it in another hundred years or so), but whether someone who believes in fundamental principle as well as daily practice that sexuality is evil can really enter a contract for a sustained sexual union seems to me to be quite dubious. The puritan who will not give up his puritanism or will not even try to give it up is more than a little mad, I think. And given what we have come to believe marriage is, his capacity for marriage must be considered minimal indeed.

But the convinced puritans are not as much a

problem as the partial, reluctant puritanical aspects of our own personalities that still affect us. The puritan strain in us is such a marvelous excuse; it justifies, rationalizes, and reinforces no-saying. It underwrites our little acts of meanness and vindictiveness. It makes us feel guilty about our hesitant attempts to be playful, and urges us to quit when these attempts are not immediately successful. It strengthens our shame, our fear, our anxieties, our self-loathing, our disgust. It argues vigorously about our responsibilities, our commitments, about the seriousness of life. It shrugs its shoulders and says, "Well, after all, sex isn't everything." (Although no one ever claimed that it was.)

Puritanism will persist as long as fear of sex persists. It has been dealt a decisive blow by contemporary psychology and some of the more recent theological reflection on that psychology. Human history is not all circle; progress does occur, and we have made progress against puritanism. It would have been impossible even ten years ago for someone within Catholic Christianity to write a book of theological reflections on sexual playfulness. (It's still a bit risky, but by and large safe.) It would be foolish to think that puritanism will release its clammy grip on Christianity without a fight. It may take several more generations before liberation from puritanism will have been substantially accomplished. In the meantime we will have to put up with a good deal of nonsense about sexual revolutions, sexual permissiveness, and the new sexuality. Much of this nonsense, incidentally, is in reality cryptopuritanism, attempting to impose a whole new set of sexual obligations to replace the old. The hedonist's injunction, "enjoy, enjoy," is as absolutely moralistic as the puritan's, "deny, deny."

The defeat of puritanism will not mean, as such half-witted utopian visions as *The Harrod Experiment* would have us believe, that the human race can enjoy sex without fear. For sex without fear would be sex without passion and that would be no sex at all. The goal is rather more modest and more realistic: sex without unreasonable or inappropriate fear, sex that is enjoyable, playful, rewarding, festive, fantastic, and funny, and sex which at the same time recognizes its own demonic and ecstatic dimensions. It is precisely that which gives sex its mystery, its depth, its power, and its strength that also makes it frightening. Between the hedonism that sees only delight and the puritanism that sees only terror there ought to be a middle path that sees both terror and delight, with delight strong enough to laugh at terror and thereby make it even delightful. You won't find that middle course through Harrod experiments or sexual communes or wife-swapping. You will only get it through slow, patient development of skills, insights, and understanding in the sexual game. And that, to repeat once again the basic theme of this volume, is a lifelong task.

chapter 10

Love is play; play is love. Both defy death.

Just as children only play with those who are friends, so sexual partners only play with those they love. Love precedes play and follows it. It makes possible the atmosphere of trust, confidence, of festivity, fantasy, and wit that is essential for play to begin. Play, in turn, enhances all these characteristics in a common life together. You can, it would seem, love someone intensely and not be playful. Parents can have a deep and abiding love for a child and still resist all inclinations to play with that child. In principle, I suppose that such a relationship between parent and child is not wrong, but not to play with a child when the spontaneous impulses of both the adult

and childish natures would lead you to that playfulness is, to say the least, rather strange. Your
relationship with the child may still be a good
one, but there is something missing.

Similarly, it is possible to have a good relationship with a spouse without the lightness, the
laughter, the teasing, the jokes, the surprises that
constitute play. Certainly there are many married
people with good relationships whose sexual lives
are serious, restrained, utterly devoid of playfulness. Again, there is nothing "wrong" with such
marriages, but something is missing.

Playfulness reinforces love, but love does not
necessarily generate playfulness, although there
is a spontaneous impulse in that direction once
love is permitted freedom. It is the thought of
death, explicit or implicit, which inhibits love and
restrains playfulness.

Father Ladislaus Boros notes (in *Hidden God,*
Seabury Press, 1973) that to love means to say,
"You will not die."

> Love confers immortality upon the beloved
> human being. . . . It cannot be that you will
> leave me forever. It cannot be that you are
> given over to eternal destruction. It cannot
> be that there can be never again the possi-
> bility of your developing into that which I
> saw in moments of inner vision. . . . Faith in
> the immortality of the loved one is not so
> much the result of logical deduction as the
> inner evidence of friendship itself. . . . In
> human friendship there is an archetypal proof

that needs no further proof for human love—
the presence of the friend, the opportunity of
a limitless unfolding before him, and the
presence of the Absolute which makes all this
possible. . . . Friendship makes clear the un-
shakable soul-shattering presence of absolute
goodness.

It is in this death-defying component of love
that playfulness takes its origin. If no evil power,
however strong, can overcome love, then there
is no reason not to play. The refusal to play is a
hedging of the bet. We will love, yes, but we will
keep some restrictions, some restraints and controls on that love as a hedge against the tragedy
of its coming to an end. In a world dominated by
evil, suffering, and death there is little about which
to be playful. Play in such circumstances is childish, frivolous, and irresponsible. Ironic and sar-
donic laughter is permitted, but joyous merriment
is foolish and self-deceptive. There is, after all,
relatively little to laugh about if death simply
means oblivion.

Obviously, most people do not think these
things explicitly. I am talking not about a conscious process of thought and emotion that goes
on in a sustained sexual relationship but about the
psychological and existential dynamics through
which people make their choices. The choice can
be light or heavy, comic or tragic, hopeful or des-
pairing. In a universe in which neither alternative
of each pair is self-evident, the choice is rarely
made in so many words. We make it, rather, by

the way we live, by the little risks we do or do not take, the little opportunities we seize or do not seize, the little chances we grab as they float by or ignore without a second glance. The fundamental option that guides our life is made slowly and gradually. We see it forming a pattern for our life only when we look back. We do not simply exercise a fundamental option for or against playfulness, for or against hope, for or against laughter on any given day. It is the small choices, the drift as well as the decision, that determine that fundamental choice. We move from predisposition to fundamental option without being very clear about what we are doing. We discover our choice only when its inevitable long-term effects are so obvious that we can ignore them no longer.

Resentment, self-pity, the imposition of obligations on the other are characteristics of a non-playful sexual relationship. We develop a long list of the things that the other has done and the burdens we have had to tolerate. We feel terribly sorry for all the things we had to put up with, and seek consolation from others who will agree (if only to escape) with us. The resentments rooted in self-pity are precious. They give meaning and purpose to our life; they organize the phenomena of experience. To lose them would be to lose an important part of the self. Yet we never make a decision to go down the path of self-pity and resentment; we simply know that when we are at the end of the path we discover that we have been walking on it for a long, long time.

We can make our relationships ones of formal exchange and barter. "I will do this if you will do that." We can even institutionalize these arrangements in formal marriage contracts, like some defiant, progressive young people do, and specify the obligations and responsibilities each partner will assume in the marriage. But the mutual obligation approach to marriage need not be explicit or formal, and in most cases it is not. In fact, those who are locked into that style are frequently surprised when they are told that their marriage is nothing more than a system of mutual obligation. They never decided to make it that, and yet they surely and inevitably made a long series of decisions leading to a network of mutual obligations binding them in a constricted and inhibited relationship. There is no way that the light touch of playfulness, with its gratuitousness, its triviality, its spontaneity, its apparent foolishness, can loosen the bonds of mutual obligation. The essence of play is that one doesn't have to do it but decides on the spur of the moment to have some fun. When play is codified, regimented, regulated, defined, it stops being play. (I do not deny the insight of social theorists, like George Casper Homens and Peter Blau, who see intimacy as an exchange relationship. Exchange there surely is, but there must be something more besides. Even Homens and Blau stop short of viewing such exchange in terms of strict classical economics.)

The self-pity-resentment style and the obligation style are both familiar modalities of contemporary marriage. In these two modalities there is not room for playfulness. Indeed it is probably the case that most contemporary American marriages that are not playful stop short of it because they are caught in the self-pity or obligation or both styles of marriage. Thus do the powers death and despair constrain and restrict our fundamental life options without our ever having quite the insight to see how they are doing it.

Only when something catches us up short, only when some sort of dramatic event forces us to review the pattern of our life and to see the shape of our fundamental options do we see how far we have come and in what direction. Only in that revelation can we grasp the options we have chosen to exclude. It is for most of us not a pleasant experience.

But options can be modified and even changed. It is never too late to start over. Indeed, starting over is of the essence of life, and we are only truly dead when we have lost our capacity for beginning again. Every day is or can be a new beginning. No matter how long a relationship has lasted, no matter what direction it has moved in, no matter what fundamental options and their resultant styles have dominated our relationship, it is still possi-

ble to begin anew. It cannot be done without reference to what has gone before, but with relative
freedom from its inevitability. One is never too
old to grow, to change. It gets harder, but we can
do it. Our relationships can begin to be playful
even today, and if there is any life or vitality left
at all, the spontaneous impulses that leap from
love to playfulness can be revived. As long as we
have not become so deadly serious (and that is to
say, dead) that we cannot laugh at ourselves, then
we can play. The first step in beginning to play is
to laugh at oneself, or, to put it differently, when
we resolve not to take ourself so damn seriously
we have begun to break the constraints of resentment, self-pity and obligation. After that anything
can happen.

And there, of course, is the problem. What will
happen when anything can happen? We have no
way of knowing. Bad things as well as good things,
perhaps. We maintain rigid control of our lives
because we are afraid that if we don't something
may happen—death may happen. To avoid that
possibility we exclude the playfulness, the pleasure, the joy that may also occur when we open
ourselves to the "anything may happen" situation.

Death will happen anyhow. The question is
whether we will go through life in constant terror
of it, or whether we can go through life laughing
at it because we believe we will conquer that
terror. If we are not willing to laugh at death and

all its surrogates, then we will flee from beginning over again, starting anew, seizing the second chance.

Strangely enough, the experience of starting over again, of rediscovering one another, is one of such special delight that it is astonishing that a man or woman should consider it difficult. These delights are not available to those starting fresh. The mystery of discovery and the discovery of mystery are intensely more pleasurable when we share them with an old friend suddenly become new again.

But starting over seems to be painful for most. One must give death to the illusions, deceptions, pretenses, and styles of relating that have become as natural as the air we breathe. We must give death to the illusion that we need not change, that we must fear change, and that we must fear to begin to change. It is indeed the fear of death that prevents us from beginning again, because beginning again is a form of death.

Hence the ultimate question: What comes after death? Annihilation? Something else? Or Some One else? Every new beginning is a death and resurrection. When a man and woman decide to restructure their relationship they are running a risk of encountering nothingness. It is truly dying. Yet they may discover someone, a lover with whom to play in sexual intimacy. For the Christian man and woman it is a foretaste, a hint of the Lover with whom we expect to play for all eternity.

Sexual play is a reflection of the playing of the Word and the Spirit that gave birth to the cosmos. It is an anticipation of the endless play of the life after resurrection. In the Christian world-view sexual play is either both of those things or a monstrous deception. As Father Boros points out, once one is swept up by the game, one has no doubts. It is more real than anything else; it is the *realest* thing there is: it is an Anticipation of the Absolute.